Saigon to Pleiku

Saigon to Pleiku

*A Counterintelligence Agent in
Vietnam's Central Highlands,
1962–1963*

David Grant Noble

McFarland & Company, Inc., Publishers
Jefferson, North Carolina

All photographs are by the author

Library of Congress Cataloguing-in-Publication Data

Names: Noble, David Grant, author.
Title: Saigon to Pleiku : a counterintelligence agent in Vietnam's central highlands, 1962-1963 / David Grant Noble.
Other titles: Counterintelligence agent in Vietnam's central highlands, 1962-1963
Description: Jefferson, North Carolina : McFarland & Company, Inc., Publishers, 2020 | Includes index.
Identifiers: LCCN 2020040253 | ISBN 9781476683737 (paperback : acid free paper) ∞
ISBN 9781476641492 (ebook)
Subjects: LCSH: Vietnam War, 1961-1975—Military intelligence—United States—History. | Noble, David Grant. | United States. Army. Counter Intelligence Corps Detachment, 704th—Biography. | Vietnam War, 1961-1975—Personal narratives, American. | Pleiku (Vietnam)—History—20th century.
Classification: LCC DS559.8.M44 N63 2020 | DDC 959.704/38 [B]—dc23
LC record available at https://lccn.loc.gov/2020040253

British Library cataloguing data are available

ISBN (print) 978-1-4766-8373-7
ISBN (ebook) 978-1-4766-4149-2

Front cover images: *left to right* David Noble standing next to a U.S. plane that crashed in the Catecka tea fields; A street scene in Pleiku showing vendors, a Montagnard with his woven burden basket, and off-duty Vietnamese soldiers; Montagnard women walking along the road to Pleiku carrying burden baskets

Printed in the United States of America

McFarland & Company, Inc., Publishers
  Box 611, Jefferson, North Carolina 28640
  www.mcfarlandpub.com

Acknowledgments

I am deeply indebted to my mother, Louise McLanahan Noble, for saving all the letters I wrote home from Vietnam and sending them to me before she died. Colonel Kumar of the Indian army, with whom I became friends in Saigon, gave me a broader perspective of the war in Vietnam. The Jarai and Bahnar people of Vietnam's Central Highlands taught me, by their very presence, about the dignity of all human beings, whatever their social and cultural background or level of economic development. My sister Alexandra Heller read developing versions of the manuscript and assured me of its value and that a publisher surely would be interested. My friend Krista Elrick helped me repeatedly with digital and computer complexities. Barbara Feller-Roth assisted me editorially, from missing commas to narrative organization and the blending of letter excerpts with memoir. Ruth Meria Noble did the proofreading.

Table of Contents

Table of Contents

Part III

Preface

While I was in college in the late 1950s, my interest in American politics and international affairs was near invisible. With no radio or television, it took events such as *Sputnik*, the Berlin Crisis, and the Kennedy-Nixon campaign to get me to a newsstand. In those years, to be uninvolved in politics was not unusual on college campuses; of course, with the draft and the military buildup in South Vietnam a few years later, this dramatically changed.

One personal political incident, however, sticks in my memory. It was early one morning in the fall of 1957. I was hunched over a textbook in a reading room, cramming for an upcoming test, when I heard a commotion near the room's entrance. Clearly, some thoughtless people were ignoring the "Quiet please!" sign on the door. I was trying to focus on my work when I suddenly heard a commanding—though not unfriendly and not unfamiliar—voice behind me say, "Wake up there, young man!" I swiveled around to find former President Harry S Truman gazing down on me. He smiled mirthfully—a gotcha moment!—then turned and strode out of the room to continue his early morning constitutional, Secret Service agents scurrying to keep up. Truman, I learned, was on campus as a visiting fellow. Did my brief encounter with the former leader of the free world spur me to attend one of his seminars, or join the Political Union? No. But later, my apathy to politics vanished. Vietnam did that.

In April 1962, only nine months after graduating from college, I was in the army stationed at Fort Holabird, Maryland, and received orders to report to a classified counterintelligence unit in Saigon. So unprepared was I for such an assignment that my first move was to the fort library to find out where Vietnam was.

Not surprisingly, the twelve months I spent in Saigon and Pleiku were very intense and personally formative; even after the passage of years, those experiences remained strong and vivid in my mind. Memorable, too, was the decade that followed my military service, when America's cities and campuses erupted in controversy over Vietnam, and a Stop-the-War movement was born, gained strength, and, finally, helped end the war.

In Pleiku, where I spent most of my tour, I was a young, greenhorn special agent trying to collect intelligence that would help America support what we were led to believe was a struggling democracy fighting an aggressive communist dictatorship. Six-foot-two and blond, I was supposed to be operating undercover. At the time, I thought what I was doing was important; of course, history proved that wrong. My reports from the Central Highlands, a territory inhabited by more than thirty indigenous tribes known collectively as Montagnards, were, indeed, informative to headquarters in Saigon; but they changed nothing in the long run. On the other hand, what I did and experienced in Vietnam had importance at another level: I began to learn about the world, and where I stood in relation to American foreign policy, and, of course, the real nature of the Vietnam War.

It was my luck that I served very early in the war—before the Bay of Tonkin, and before so many young Americans and many more Vietnamese perished or were maimed. My time there in 1962 and 1963 is a period about which the American public generally knows little. Army intelligence-gathering activities in the Central Highlands are even less well-known. They were secret then and remain obscure today. More than half a century later, in one army archive after another, I have tried to gain access to the Intelligence reports I wrote from Pleiku, and, in every case, ran into a stone wall: no trace or no interest, it seems.

The following pages contain only *my* story—what *I* did and what happened to *me*. They do not pretend to be *the* story, whatever that may be. What I've written includes both memoir and excerpts from letters I wrote home while I was in Vietnam. These my mother saved—about sixty of them—and sent to me before she died in 2002. The following narrative casts some light on a thin slice of military history, but it is also a coming-of-age story about a naive, inexperienced, youth who, under demanding circumstances, learned something about himself and about life. It follows his journey from a believer in his country's policies to a dissenter.

I wrote this story not only because I needed to, but also because every aspect, however small, of this unfortunate war should be brought to light. I was twenty-two when I went to Vietnam. Now I am eighty-one. Like many octogenarians, I spend no little time in reflection; but the words in the following pages are not the nostalgic (or guilty) memories of an old man. I drafted this narrative when the experiences were still relatively fresh and vivid. As to the letters, they were written almost in real time, usually within twenty-four or forty-eight hours of when the events occurred. So, too, for my accounts included in Part III, of the anti-war rallies and marches I joined later in the sixties. To protect their and their families' privacy, I have changed some names; they are Gordon Gallagher, Mike Smith, Robert Kuhn, Kumar, Nelson, Don, and Jake. To keep their authenticity, the excerpts from my letters are reproduced as originally written, without editing. As to the photographs, especially of the Montagnards, I hope they convey, with some immediacy, a feeling for the dignity

Portrait of a Montagnard of the Bahnar tribe, near Pleiku, 1962.

and beauty of these indigenous people, who were caught in the middle of terrible events that were far beyond their control, and who suffered much.

We know about what happened in the past mostly through the writings of professional historians. We know less about our history from the stories of individuals who participated in it. Often, those personal stories get lost: not, I hope, this one.

3

PART I

Memory

May 12, 1962, early afternoon. It was stifling hot and oppressively humid when I stepped off my Pan American flight and crossed the tarmac into Saigon's Tan Son Nhut airport. Twelve months later, as I watched the coastline around Da Nang vanish below a bank of clouds, Vietnam became memory, for me at least.

Memory—how does it work? As years flow by, do memories dim like a mural in the sun? Do we recall only what touched us emotionally? For sure, there is a selection process at work, about which we understand little.

When I was a child in bed at night, I would squeeze my eyes shut and evoke patchwork patterns of vivid colors that trembled across the dark cosmos of my mind. Tiny blue dots streamed toward me from a great distance, like stars, only to metamorphose into a sharp shimmering pattern of green and yellow before spinning off into darkness. Then I would walk into the memory place. It was a vast library with many aisles and sliding ladders reaching into balconies. Thousands of small drawers were set in the walls of the library, each holding a slip of paper inscribed with a memory.

The archive was run by a wizened gnome whose job it was to retrieve memories. A diminutive old fellow, he would scurry indefatigably down aisles, up ladders, and along balconies in a ceaseless search for particular drawers whose contents had been requested. When he found the one he needed, he would pull out its memory and hurry back to the operations center to process it. He worked with speed and dexterity, barely able to keep pace with the endless stream of demands placed upon him.

And so I believe memories do not fade: rather, they hide in a drawer waiting to be retrieved. To be sure, over time, some compartments empty and trivial data vanish. But the important slips of paper remain in place, written in indelible ink. So it is with me and Vietnam, and this memoir.

5

Part I

By now, of course, so many years later, not a few of the library's drawers are empty, but others still contain their notes. Some of my memories are static, like pictures; others replay like a video. Reviewing them now, I journey halfway across the world and encounter a youth, by now nearly a stranger, but a nascent version of whom I became.

The gnome has support—photographs, made in Saigon and the Central Highlands, Montagnard country. I started with my mother's Zeiss Ikon rangefinder, dating to around 1929. She was a talented photographer in her own right and filled scrapbooks with carefully annotated black-and-white pictures of her family. When I left home for Vietnam, she gave it to me—the passing of the camera. Then, after I came back, I too made albums.

Before she died, in 2002, my mother sent me a box filled with correspondence I had mailed home forty years before—fifty-seven letters, postcards too, handwritten or typed, containing accounts of experiences, places, and people. She had lovingly tied them up with a string and put them in order by date received. Some she had even retyped and circulated to my brother and sisters. I'm sure, if the Internet had existed then, she would have looked up the weather every day in Saigon and Pleiku. As for me, I had completely forgotten about writing letters home, and for some reason ten more years passed before I read them. When I did, I was amazed to find detailed descriptions of events I had only fuzzily remembered. Since I was in Intelligence and functioning in a (supposedly) covert status, it was good the army wasn't then censoring outgoing mail.

What surprised me more, in some cases to the point of embarrassment, was to see how candidly I wrote about what I did and thought and felt. Who wrote this? I often thought. Was it really me? Do I still know this person?

But before returning to Saigon, I probably should set the stage.

Becoming an
Intelligence Agent

After graduating from college in 1961, I was expecting every day to find a letter in the mail from the draft board. Ten years at private elite boarding schools and university had instilled in me a need to experience what I thought would be the "real" world. Whereas my college friends were heading for officer candidate school, graduate school, or the newly formed Peace Corps, I let myself be drafted into the army as an ordinary private. While waiting for the draft notice, I drove to Montana with a friend to find work. Early one Monday morning, we were standing first in line at the labor office in Dillon when a rancher drove up and looked us over. He said he was Earl Van Deren and needed hay hands to work on his cattle ranch located along the Beaverhead River. Eight dollars a day plus room and board for five or six weeks. We enthusiastically accepted and followed him to the ranch where he asked for my car keys, saying I could get them back on Saturday after work.

Ranch life in Montana's Beaverhead Valley was a far cry from Yale University. We worked long hours in the hot sun six days a week and I nearly forgot about the army. But then one evening, the rancher's wife knocked on the door of the bunkhouse where we were staying and handed me an envelope from the Selective Service. When I mentioned the letter at the dinner table, the rancher quipped, "Don't worry, Dave, after this job the army will be a walk in the park."

After passing my physical in Boston, a friend told me about the army's Counterintelligence Corps. He said if I enlisted and was accepted in the CIC, my chances would be good to attend the army's renowned language school in Monterey, California. I already spoke fluent French and figured that, with Russian under my belt, I could later apply for a job in the Foreign Service. This was 1961. It was during the Cold War and the Berlin

7

Crisis. French was still considered the language of diplomacy, but Russian was the language to learn. I had a plan.

That winter, I went through ten weeks of basic training at Fort Dix, New Jersey, then was accepted into Intelligence school at Fort Holabird, Maryland. The plan was working, so far. I should note, however, that my last two years in college had been a struggle academically, especially writing a senior thesis on the novels of Emil Zola, and I had not been closely following current affairs. In fact, I hardly kept up with the news and was unaware that President Kennedy was building a cadre of military advisors to support a struggling new government in Southeast Asia—in a place called South Vietnam.

Excerpt from a letter to my parents, February 21, 1962:

> ... This is definitely a high pressure school.... If boot camp was physically tiring, this present routine is equally fatiguing mentally. However, it is getting more interesting than it was at the beginning and I am learning quite a bit.
>
> The Army has its own way when it comes to teaching as when it comes to everything else. Every syllable of verbal content which is disseminated to the class is highly organized and planned, so it seems. In a given amount of time, a given amount of facts must be expressed and the Army seems to know just how much of the one can fit within the other. At the end of the day one feels as if he has been in front of a high-powered machine gun only he hopes that some of the bullets have not gone in one side and out the other, as it were.
>
> My classes consist of map reading, legal principles (constitutional and military law), interrogations, investigations, security regulations, Army organization, and the like. There will be increasing practical work (interviews, mock POW captures, tailing) and decreasing class lectures. We have already begun interviewing ... there is a group of professional actors from Baltimore who assume the role of interviewees of various types. These actors are fantastic, and create all sorts of situations which we the interrogators must adjust to. Some of it is very amusing, especially if you're not the one on the stand!

My parents were planning a trip to Washington, D.C., and wanted to stop to see me at Fort Holabird on their way. In a letter dated February 21, I told them, "Feel free to drive into the Fort if you want to have a look around ... it's very small, an open post. Retreat is sounded at about that time [5:00] so if you're driving around and hear a bugle, stop the car and get out and wait till it's over (as if the national anthem were playing). I mention this because it's a strict regulation and there are apt to be many top brass walking around."

In another letter home, written at about the same time, I informed them that "unfortunately, language school is a very remote possibility for me. There simply are almost no openings left for our group. This is disappointing. But I might still get a good overseas assignment." Fact was, the only language opening was in Serbo-Croatian, a language I had never heard of. So, when assignment-preference forms were passed out, I wrote France as my first choice. Then I wondered what other French-speaking countries there were where we had army bases. Belgium? I put down Belgium. As to a third choice, I was stuck, so I scribbled "any other French-speaking country." That's how I learned that French was spoken in Vietnam.

A couple of weeks later, our class gathered in an auditorium to be told our duty stations. When the sergeant called my name, he paused, and instead of announcing the name of a city, he said a number. Afterward, I asked him what it meant. "Saigon," was his reply. Noticing the blank look on my face, he added, "Vietnam." Vietnam I knew of but had trouble placing it. That evening, I went to Fort Holabird's library where, in its sole world atlas, I could find no "Vietnam" in the index. The librarian suggested I try "Indochina" and there it was, along with Tonkin, Annam, and Cochinchina. To find out that the army intelligence center's atlas was so out-of-date was my first hint of things to come.

In April 1962, I graduated and received my credentials as a special agent in the CIC. While awaiting my orders, an "official" passport, and tropical disease inoculations, I was assigned menial tasks—mopping and buffing floors, cleaning latrines, and "policing" the grounds. One day I learned that army rules forbid being assigned work below one's military occupational specialty (MOS), and after bringing this to the attention of a superior, I was sent to the library to read about Vietnam. Books about Vietnam? I found only a slim volume of Vietnamese poetry and a pamphlet. The poems, translated into English, told of lovers separated by war and young women grieving over the loss of their sweethearts. I found them deeply moving. The enemies, to my surprise, were Chinese.

The pamphlet had been produced years before for the benefit of naval officers assigned to Saigon's embassy. It offered tips about what clothing to bring to the tropics, the appropriate dress code for various official and social functions, and (most importantly) how to gain membership in Le Club Sportif, an elite Saigon spa for French colonials that allowed admittance to military officers. Again, I was surprised by Holabird's lack of even basic information about Vietnam. Then I thought, maybe that's why I'm going—to fill in some blanks.

I did find books to read about Vietnam elsewhere, however: *The Quiet American*, by Graham Green, for example (then banned in Vietnam), and

Part I

The Ugly American, by William J. Lederer and Eugene Burdick. I scoured the *New York Times* every day for mention of South Vietnam and sometimes found short articles buried deep inside; they concerned incidents of guerrilla attacks and U.S. military advisors. I asked one of my Holabird instructors how to prepare for Vietnam, and he recommended I learn about Crazy Horse, Che Guevara, and Vo Nguyen Giap, the Viet Minh hero of Dien Bien Phu.

One day I was summoned to G-2, the Intelligence building, where a first lieutenant handed me my orders, classified "secret," and gave me travel instructions. I was to go to Travis Air Force Base in California and from there fly by Military Air Transport Service (MATS) to Saigon to join the 704th Intelligence Corps Detachment. I was told to buy civilian clothes (cost to be reimbursed in Saigon) and, if asked, say I was an interpreter attached to the military—deep cover. When the lieutenant was done, he asked if I had any questions.

"One, Sir—what do I do when I arrive in Saigon?" He smiled and gave me a knowing look from across his desk. "Don't worry, Noble, you'll be met." A shiver ran up my spine. Saigon was awaiting the arrival of "008," *Saigon*—even the word had a certain ring.

Excerpt from a letter to my parents, April 6, 1962:

I have more news. And it's good. I fly from S.F. on May 10th. And I will probably be able to get 13 days travel time to get there. This means leaving Ft. Holabird on the 27th. But, of course, I could almost walk there in 13 days so I expect to get home for a few days before leaving. At this time, I'll bring home my car and arrange my affairs (i.e. clean my desk, etc.!!)

I'll be traveling under classified orders so I cannot say very much.... I'll have a civilian passport and papers and will pretend to be a civilian. And I'll be able to bring 100 lbs. of civ. clothes with me. The type of civilian I'll pose as pulls in a salary considerably greater than a pvt., so I imagine that my standard of living will correspond somewhat. Can you imagine such a deal? (Not that I'm getting a raise—).

Honolulu and the
Waikikian

At Travis, I hooked up with three other special agents also headed for the 704th—all Intelligence neophytes like me. They were young too and had never been to the Far East. Nor did they speak any language known in Vietnam. We were told that our flight from Travis was canceled and we would depart from San Francisco the next day. Unable to afford a hotel in the city, we took a taxi to the Presidio, flashed our new credentials, and were directed to the post's bachelor officers' quarters (BOQ). My second cover—now I was an army officer, more or less.

We were determined to make the most of our last night in the States. At a spacious high-ceilinged bar with sawdust on the floor and a ragtime band, we downed a few beers and got acquainted with one another. Waitresses in scant outfits, black net stockings, and lace garters took turns swooping over our heads on a swing. After that, a cabby took us to a late-hours joint where, given our limited budget, we sullenly drank what we figured would be our final beers in America.

In Honolulu, we had a maintenance layover during which we were to be guests of Pan American at the Waikikian, a beachfront resort hotel in Honolulu. Uniforms, barracks, and military rank were now a thing of the recent past. How long could this streak of luck go on?

Excerpt from a letter to my parents, May 15, 1962:

Another few hours and we land in Saigon. Due to the continual time changes of the past three days, none of us have much idea what time it really is. Today I'm having two breakfasts ... one at 5:00 A.M Guam time, another an hour later at 7:00 A.M Saigon time. Dinner last night was at the same time as my normal EST breakfast, and now I'm told it was 2 days ago since we jumped from Thursday—Saturday! Confused? I am!!

Our flight [from Travis] was canceled and we were placed on a Pan Am commercial jet which left Frisco on the 10th at 9:00 a.m. The four of us stayed up till

Part I

4:00 nightclubbing and got up at 6:00 a.m. with a hangover. We arrived in Honolulu at 11:00 a.m. and left there last night at 1:00 a.m. (so we had 14 hours in Hawaii). Pan Am put us up in a really top notch hotel (The Waikikian) and treated us like kings. Of course, we went to the beach for the day and swam and dined on the terrace under the palms watching the natives surf board.

We were a disparate foursome: Tony Brush, a dark-haired, genial guy from Tennessee; Jake, a tall, good-looking, smooth-talking, working-class Philadelphian who projected worldly experience and cynicism; Don, soft and clumsy, black-rimmed glasses, affecting self-importance to camouflage a lack of self-assurance. At the hotel, we bought bathing suits, walked a few yards to the beach, and swam in the warm Pacific, sunned, and drank mai tais.

Excerpt from a letter to my parents dated May 20, 1962:

...A GI whom I got to know on the plane coming over here told me, over a drink at our beachfront hotel on Waikiki, all about the CIC. He said it stood for the Civil Information Committee and was undercover stuff with spies and so forth and how no one knew their real identity. "For example," he said, "you could be CIC agents working undercover right now checking up on me." As you can imagine, I almost died not laughing aloud. I stuck my head in my beer and drank deeply and then coughed out my laughter. I ran into him again in Saigon and had a little trouble explaining that my translator's job hadn't quite panned out and that I was now with Central Registry.

I had an uncle and aunt who had gone to Honolulu on their honeymoon in 1938. After the Japanese attack on Pearl Harbor, he joined the navy and spent the next two decades in the Office of Naval Intelligence, the navy's counterpart to the CIC. They were very surprised to get my call, and my uncle, George X. McLanahan, came to the Waikikian that evening to join Tony and me for a drink. Next, we drove to his house high in the hills to join the family for cocktails. They lived in a large white stucco house with a beautiful view. He told me it was marked on the maps of the Japanese pilots to help guide them to Pearl Harbor. He and my aunt then treated Tony and me to a sumptuous dinner and Polynesian floor show at one of Honolulu's historic beachfront hotels. With polished worldliness (no doubt, to show his young unworldly nephew how things were done), he slipped generous tips to every doorman and waiter who attended to us. It was a memorable send-off after which they dropped us off at the hotel around ten with a wish for luck in whatever lay ahead.

Back in our room, Tony and I discovered that Jake was missing. Following a hasty search of the hotel premises, we found him spread-eagled on his back on the beach, dead drunk and acutely sunburned. We got him on his feet and half carried, half dragged him to our room, where we discussed what to do. The bus back to the airport was to depart shortly. I proposed leaving him in the room to figure things out in the morning. Tony, however, wisely pointed out that we were listed on the same orders and would be considered responsible for one another. Besides, the colonel in charge of our flight had a passenger roster. We had to work fast. Tony and I sat Jake under a cold shower, slapped his cheeks, shook his arms, and yelled at him. Slowly, he came around, although in a mean temper. While we worked on him, Don went for black coffee, plenty of it.

By departure time, Jake had improved enough that we could get him dressed. With two of us propping him up, we managed to board him on the bus. At the airport, we steered him across the tarmac, up the ramp, onto the plane, and into a seat. When a fellow passenger asked what was ailing him, I said it was food poisoning.

We napped intermittently during the long leg to Saigon. We'd been ordered to keep our briefcases with us at all times as they contained our classified orders. At some point during the flight I heard Don call the stewardess and loudly ask her to keep an eye on his briefcase while he went to the lavatory. "It contains secret documents," he said. A ripple of chuckles could be heard from nearby passengers. Tony and I looked at each other in mortification. Jake was asleep. So, among us four, we had a drunk and an idiot. Once again, I wondered what lay in store.

Arrival in Vietnam

It was early afternoon when we landed at Tan Son Nhut Airport and showed our maroon government passports to military officials. We glanced around the terminal for our welcome committee. "Don't worry, Noble, you'll be met" replayed in my mind as our fellow passengers dispersed. Save for a pair of military police, the four of us soon found ourselves alone in the bleak terminal building standing uneasily by our luggage. It was hot, stifling hot, and humid, and I was still dressed for the chill fog of San Francisco.

After a while, one of the MPs sauntered over and asked if he could be of assistance. We assured him we were fine and just waiting to be picked up. Another quarter of an hour passed. Now, except for us, the airport was empty. We found a bench and waited. We did not know where to go, we did not know a soul, and we had no phone number to call in case of a problem. Even the name of our unit on our orders was stamped SECRET. With the military police keeping a watchful eye on us, a feeling of dread crept into my gut as I began to face a reality: no one was going to meet us and we had no backup plan and little money. In short, we were stuck and didn't know what to do.

In a minute, I thought, I'll wake up.

The two military policemen showed up again and this time told us curtly to accompany them. They led us to the police station at the far end of the terminal. I imagined sending a telegram home: *safe arrival Saigon stop charged with loitering stop.* At the station, the police captain demanded our passports and asked what we were doing in Saigon. By now, it was obvious we needed official assistance, so I handed him my passport, CIC credentials, and classified orders. Half an hour in Saigon and my cover blown. The captain shook his head, rolled his eyes, and made some other gestures of dismay. Then he picked up his phone. He worked his way through a telephonic maze until, finally, he reached someone at the 704th

Intelligence Corps Detachment and said he was holding four lost and disoriented special agents at the airport. With a sad look, he told us to wait outside—someone would come to collect us.

Half an hour later, a black Chevy sedan pulled up to the curb. The driver, a handsome fellow in his thirties with neatly combed black hair, introduced himself as Captain Nelson—"Mr." Nelson. More deep cover, apparently. We loaded our bags into the trunk and were driven to a small compound located in a quiet residential neighborhood two blocks off the main avenue that led from Tan Son Nhut Airport to downtown Saigon. Mr. Nelson stopped at a solid metal gate, opened it, and drove into a tree-shaded courtyard where another black sedan and two military jeeps, both painted black, were parked in the driveway. To the right, in the courtyard, I caught sight of a rhesus monkey secured to the end of a chain that was attached to the trunk of a tree. Beyond, also shaded by tropical trees, was a two-story, stucco, French-colonial style villa. It bridged an open veranda to a second building. The rest of the compound was enclosed by high block walls topped with cemented glass shards.

Leaving our luggage outside, we entered the main house and found ourselves in a room with several people working at desks. There, we were told to wait. The person nearest introduced himself: his name was Bob Headley, the outfit's translator. Next, beyond him, we were introduced to Captain Hamel, the operations officer. Hamel had dark hair, too, and a pencil moustache, and he gave the impression of a man who spent much time behind a desk. He remarked on the obvious—that they had not been informed when we would arrive. A sign indicated that Nelson's desk was to the left of Hamel's; this was the space where the officers worked. Eventually, a burly, round-shouldered, middle-age man with close-cropped graying hair appeared in a doorway to the right of the other officers' desks. He was the commander. He looked us over silently, and then motioned us to follow him to a front section of the room, where he took a seat at a table and silently read our orders. Through the window behind him, I noticed that the monkey had climbed to the lower limb of his tree, his chain looped down.

The commander glanced up from our papers and brusquely motioned us to be seated. He introduced himself as Major Gordon Gallagher. He'd been expecting us, he said, but had not been notified of our arrival time. I was learning something new every minute. As background, he informed us that General Maxwell Taylor (Chairman of the Joint Chiefs) had visited Saigon late the previous year and asked General Harkins, the commander of U.S. forces, to summarize the military's counterintelligence capability. When Harkins informed him that there was none, Taylor ordered that a unilateral counterintelligence operation be established. Thus, in January, Central Registry Detachment—that was the 704th's cover name—was formed with the arrival of the six agents now stationed in Saigon and another, Jim Ishihara, who had opened a field office in the Delta. Soon after Central Registry's supposedly covert arrival, Gallagher added, a Viet Cong document had come into the possession of the Vietnamese military; the document recorded the date, time, and flight number of all the initial agents.

Gallagher told us he had specifically requested highly qualified agents. Then, looking us over with disapproval, he added, "You're what I got." He gave a helpless shrug as if wondering what to do with us.

Excerpt from a letter to my parents postmarked May 15, 1962:

> In a few weeks I may be sent "upcountry," as they call it. This will depend on my qualifications and ability. Of course this is somewhat alarming. However, my boss is a man to have great confidence in. There is nothing he doesn't know. He told us that he especially requested of the Intelligence Center that he be sent none but the highest qualified agents. I can see why now, as the situation here and especially my position are extremely sensitive.

The commander then issued us a caution: to keep to ourselves whatever opinions we might have about American involvement in Vietnam. They were irrelevant, he said, because the president had made a decision to support South Vietnam, and the military was committed to doing that. "We're in it up to here," he said, raising a hand to eye level. For myself, I hadn't yet formed an opinion about America's policy regarding Vietnam, but I sensed he had.

"Any questions?" he asked. I raised my hand and he gestured permission to speak. I said I had read a little about the Viet Cong and wasn't clear who they were. Gallagher looked amused. "The Viet Cong is the bad guy—you'll know him because he looks just like a Vietnamese." Admittedly, my question was naive; on the other hand, looking back, perhaps it went to the heart of the matter. With a brusque final word of welcome, he turned the rest of our orientation over to Nelson. Nelson was well spoken and well dressed and had a smoother, more sophisticated manner than his boss. He first informed us that we were not to refer to one another by rank and reminded us that he was "Mr. Nelson." He said he had previously served in the embassy in Saigon and spoke French. I wondered if he had read Fort Holabird's dress-code booklet and was a member of the Club

Sportif. He gave us a quick tour of the premises. The other building was a dormitory for the enlisted agents where two of us would be quartered. Unfortunately, he went on, due to space limitations, two of us would have to be lodged downtown. There and then we drew lots; Tony and I were to be cast out.

Work hours, Nelson informed us, were from seven a.m. to noon and three to six in the afternoon. Saigon natives, he remarked, took a long afternoon siesta—a decadent custom of the tropics—and since we worked with local agencies, we were obliged to do so, as well. I mentioned that I had been instructed at Fort Holabird to buy business clothes before leaving the States and to turn in my receipts for reimbursement when I arrived in Saigon. Nelson looked surprised but took the receipts and said he would discuss reimbursement later. After the meeting, he drove Tony and me to where we would be staying. It was late afternoon by now and I could barely remember when I had last eaten or slept. I was jet-lagged, as well, and felt too weary to care where I stayed. Any place, any bed would do.

Nelson drove down the main avenue to the city center while Tony and I sat silently in the back of the Chevy sedan. Along the way, we passed the presidential palace, the nerve center of the Ngo Dinh Diem regime, which recently had been bombed by dissident young Vietnamese air force officers in a failed coup d'état. As we went by, I caught sight of guards in starched white uniforms and helmets strolling about under the trees, submachine guns slung over their shoulders.

The Continental Palace

On Tu Do Street, we passed a huge French-colonial-era hotel on the left, its dining room open to the street. Above, writ large on the awning, was "Continental Palace." Whew, I thought. Impressive. Just beyond, a wide busy boulevard, Le Loi, entered on the right. As we drove around the square, Nelson pointed out the new high-rise Caravelle Hotel, where, I later discovered, foreign journalists gathered in the top-floor bar. Across from it was the National Assembly building.

Having swung completely around, Nelson pulled up at the entrance to the Continental Palace. There were elegant-looking people having drinks on the veranda and waiters in white jackets hovering around. Nelson glanced over his shoulder. "Here we are." Tony and I looked at each other in disbelief. I thought he must be jesting. From army barracks in Maryland to a resort hotel in Hawaii, and now the Continental Palace? But no, it was neither joke nor dream. This is where I would be residing.

At the front desk, we learned we were on the American plan, which included breakfast and either lunch or dinner in the restaurant. We were to write our room number on meal checks and Uncle Sam would pay. A bellboy relieved us of our bags and directed us to a metal-cage elevator beyond the front desk. I drew the door shut with a clang and pressed the third-floor button, and the vintage machine lurched into action. When it thumped to a stop, a houseboy leaped up from reed mats spread on the tiled corridor and led us down the hallway, which was open on one side and overlooked an inner courtyard. Doors to rooms were widely spaced along its inner wall, ours being at the end. We entered a bedroom that had a single four-poster bed. From this room a doorway led into the master bedroom and a double four-poster with a carved wood framework from which gracefully hung loops of mosquito netting tied up with white ribbons. A pair of free-standing armoires occupied the right-hand wall. At the front, French doors opened onto a narrow balcony overlooking the

The Continental Palace, in Saigon, viewed from atop the Caravelle Hotel.

square and National Assembly. Our suite had a spacious white-tiled bathroom appointed with wash basin, large open shower, toilet, and bidet. Hot water was not an amenity; nor was it ever desired.

Tony and I opened the French doors and gazed out over our new world. We unpacked and placed our clothes in the standing closets; there would be no footlocker inspections here. Fatigue seemed to have vanished, and we headed down to the café. On the way, I remembered something I had read in a spy novel. After all, I was a foreign agent now, on assignment. I should act like one. I returned to the room, tore the corner off a sheet of hotel stationery, and placed it on the top edge of the door of my armoire. Should someone snoop while I was away, I would find the paper on the floor when I returned. Fort Holabird had not included this trick in its curriculum.

At the café, we ordered a beer and people-watched. Some tables were spread along the sidewalk; some days later, however, due to a rash of drive-by bomb-throwing incidents, the sidewalk was closed off and patrons were restricted to the supposedly safer veranda, which was set back a few feet. Next stop was a three-course dinner in the hotel restaurant: courteous waiter, French cuisine, carafe of wine. As instructed, we signed the bill with our room number. Afterward, we strolled around the square and explored a narrow, winding shopping arcade, the Passage d'Eden, which was on Tu Do Street across from the hotel. We had last seen a bed in San Francisco, and even then, for only a couple of hours, and could stay awake no longer. Back in our suite, I found my slip of paper lying on the floor. Had my things been searched? Or had a breeze from the window blown it off? I wasn't "008" yet!

The Continental Palace was (today it's much modernized) an elegant relic of the French colonial era, when it was Saigon's premier hotel and a favorite meeting place for the elite. Scenes in *The Quiet American* were set in it. In 1962, despite its ambiance of vintage elegance, travel guides might have deleted a couple of stars. But its unpretentious grace and relaxed cordiality, which complemented Saigon's then postcolonial character, greatly appealed to me. Like Tony and me, not a few guests were residents; likewise, many café and restaurant patrons had the look of regulars. Given that for the past six months I had spent my time marching in ranks, cleaning latrines, and sleeping on a narrow cot in a barracks with twenty others, my new circumstances and implied social status—at least within the hotel—were a completely unexpected but easy adjustment. If this was not a dream, it seemed that truth could, indeed, be stranger than fiction.

The following passages, excerpted from a letter I wrote home soon after arrival, reveal a good deal more about the writer than about Saigon and the hotel. In 1962, Saigon *was*, indeed, a city of intrigue and danger and, as such, it contained all the elements to fire up a novice counterspy's active imagination, especially after warnings given us by Mr. Halligan. And fire up it did. In retrospect, some of my comments were less than considerate of my mother's concerns.

Excerpts from a letter to my parents dated May 16, 1962:

> *I am writing this during siesta.... I find that I am more than busy and for the time-being cannot keep up correspondence. My commander, an Irishman from the Bronx, said to me yesterday: "One thing anyone returning to civilian life who has worked for me cannot say is that the taxpayers didn't get their money's worth of me." And it's true. So far I have worked day and night with time out to eat and to get seven hours of sleep. Part of this is Mr. Gallagher and part of it is that there is an overwhelming volume of work to be done.*
>
> *Tony Brush and I were selected to live in the Continental Palace Hotel, reputedly the third best in Saigon. We are put up in a plush suite and are served breakfast in our rooms at six o'clock and given a three course dinner in the evenings ... all on the Army. It is an interesting hotel filled with people like us but representing other concerns. Individuals of unknown origins, disguised identity, and sinister missions enter and leave at all hours of the day and night. There are Americans, French, Italians, Czechs and others of whom I am not yet certain. Saigon is a city boiling with intrigue, and the Continental Palace is the residence of some of the characters involved. There are many native houseboys, waiters, porters, and such. Most of them are black marketeers and informants on the side. Who works for us, who for the police, who for foreign agencies, and who for the dreaded VC [Viet Cong] is questionable. So you trust no one.*
>
> *We have an 11:00 p.m. curfew and are advised not to walk around alone. The reason for these precautions was that VC and other communist intelligence networks have thoroughly infiltrated all elements in Saigon and especially in MAAG [Military Assistance Advisory Group]. So they are watching for us (only yesterday I strongly suspected I was being surveilled by two Vietnamese or Chinese) and pretty soon I expect they'll know a lot about me. I'll be a prime target for their intelligence. That is why we must be careful.*
>
> *To give a specific example, the women. They are exquisite; like lovely jungle birds, and very sexy. They wear the most provocative clothes I've ever seen, form-fitted of silk. Most of them have terrific figures and they all have beautiful long, thick, black hair which falls over their shoulders and down their backs, giving them a sort of wild appearance which sets off their natural grace and dignity.... But—the big "but," which throws a hitch in the deal—many are trained Viet Cong agents. We know this for certain, and were they not classified I would tell you details concerning this. Anyway, the bars are loaded with these Suzy Wongs, dressed in body tight silk dresses with the split up the leg. They are almost irresistible when they hold your hand, give you a free drink, stroke your cheek, smile at you, and ask you about your job. This happened to me last Sat. night. This is the biggest security problem we have. They also will (if you're important enough) lure you up to bed wherein, after some fun and a sound sleep, you awaken in Hanoi under the bright lights. So I am in a position of being able to trust almost no one. I can't tell anyone what I'm doing and, in fact, cannot even discuss it with Tony in our hotel room for fear of its being*

Part I

bugged. We set a couple of traps in our hotel room and found that within twelve hours our things had been searched. It's a bit of a lonely life as I have to beware of all associations and especially of people who are friendly to me, the latter being the clue to watch out ... a strange existence. Besides this, it is nigh on impossible to get to know the Vietnamese because of the language barrier, although my French is a great help.

They are an affectionate people, happy and relaxed looking. They hold hands and laugh and whisper to one another in foreign tones. Many are poor and live in huts on stilts in the water where they cultivate swamps. The women as well as the men work hard (at least sometimes) and carry unbelievable loads of wares. Per usual, the Americans' presence and money have somewhat corrupted them. They degrade themselves to get your dollars by pestering you unceasingly to buy all sorts of junk or change money on the black market.

Excerpt from a letter to my parents dated May 20, 1962:

... As for Saigon, a word or two more about the general situation here. You probably have read in the papers about Ho Chi Minh's birthday and "Harass Americans Day" and the grenade incidents. I expect the press will overdramatize all this. True, the VC were meant to give Americans a rough time yesterday to celebrate Ho Chi Minh's birthday. All they did, however, was to toss one bomb which killed no one. The other night they threw one into a bar, but it was a dud. The city is poten-

Saigon women in a Buddhist temple wearing the traditional *au dai*.

22

tially dangerous for me. That is, if I walk around at night alone, especially in certain places, I'm taking a big chance of being kidnapped or injured. But this is true in N.Y.C., Philly, Chicago, etc.... The solution is simply to stay at home. ...Diem, as you know, runs a highly controlled totalitarian state. Police are everywhere, and terrorism within the city is caused by infiltrators. So the hotel here is as safe as anywhere and safer than most places. This isn't to say we are not being informed upon or watched.

France's influence, at least on downtown Saigon, was apparent in the city's relatively orderly street layout and wide tree-lined boulevards. Tu Do (formerly Rue Catinat, now Dong Khoi) ran by the hotel's dining room toward the river, which was only a ten-minute walk away. It became a favorite after-dinner stroll. I passed a variety of stores, plain-looking bars, and Indian fabric shops, whose proprietors urged me to enter and see their inventories. There was also an upscale government-operated commercial arts and crafts center, which I often did enter to admire the hand-made furniture, beautiful lacquer paintings, and elaborate ivory carvings.

Eventually, I would arrive at the park along the Saigon River where Vietnamese families and young couples strolled along the cobblestone esplanade and stopped at food-cart vendors. The esplanade was wide and well lighted and had benches and small arbors with settees inside. There was no hint of political tension or war; everyone appeared relaxed and carefree. Having been raised in New England, I could not help noticing how many strollers held hands, including even pairs of young men. But after a while, I recognized this as a natural custom expressing friendship. Not surprisingly, some GIs considered it effeminate and spoke about it in derogatory terms.

As a rule, I would find a spot along the river's edge to sit and observe the promenade. What I found particularly pleasing was the soft atonal musical sound of the Vietnamese language. I was also intrigued by the exotic—to me—aromas emanating from the food carts. Occasionally I loosened up and sampled their delicacies. I also watched the sampans poling up and down the wide Saigon River, small ferries being loaded with commuters, and ships and barges as they slowly progressed upstream. Along the far shore of the river there were lights and I could make out boats and I wondered who lived over there. The river park excited all my senses, and sometimes I wished I was a native of this intriguing city rather than an outsider who understood so little. At the least, I wished I had a friend— American, French, or Vietnamese—with whom to share what I was seeing and experiencing. Little did I realize how soon this would happen. I had never been in a throng of Orientals before and, at first, felt ill at ease. But the Vietnamese never made me feel out of place, unwelcome, or like the stranger I was; of course, they had lifetimes of experience with foreigners living in their midst. Why not now Americans?

A major thoroughfare, Le Loi, approached the square by the hotel. This divided boulevard led in the direction of Cholon, Saigon's Chinese sister city. It was crowded with pedestrians, buses, taxicabs, private cars, and cyclos. Pushcarts, sales booths, shops, small Vietnamese eating places, business offices, and a movie theater lined its sidewalks. It was another favorite place for an evening stroll, especially as it led to the *marché central*, a huge covered marketplace throbbing with activity and pedestrian traffic. Much about Saigon I remember with fond nostalgia, having forgotten the distaste I initially had for some aspects of the city.

Excerpt from a letter to my brother and his wife, June 13, 1962:

... There are sections of Saigon which look like the N.G. [National Geographic] magazine photos. The bank, business, and embassy blocks are modern and western, and the center of town where I live is quite European looking. But most of the city consists of a maze of crowded streets & alleys and jumbled-up buildings and shacks. Most of the people are poor. They are dirty and ragged and lie around on the streets & sidewalks amongst all kinds of mess. They have no sense of sanitation, and I am sure much less need of it than we have. They usually go barefoot. The women carry around their wares in two baskets suspended at either end of a

A ferry loading passengers to cross the Saigon River.

cross bar which rests on their shoulders. Old women carry terrific loads. The busy streets are usually jammed full of throngs of people selling, buying, walking, bicycling, motor scooting, donkey carting, driving, yelling, etc. The odors are out of this world—almost enough to choke you. It is a world so foreign to me that I only pass through when necessary holding my breath. Today I accidently stepped on a big, half decomposed dead sewer rat, which was in the street. Then there is the good part of town where the French used to live before 1955. Spacious houses of modern French architecture sit back from tree shaded streets. My knowledge of the city is quite superficial due to the fact that I do not have the opportunity to look around much. Also, there is such a chasm between me and the ordinary Vietnamese (language, race, culture, economy) that mixing it up is hard. Since I've been here I haven't even met any French or Americans (except military). In fact, you might say that apart from my fellow workers and business contacts, I know no one. This is disappointing.

In the spring of 1962, U.S. military personnel in Vietnam numbered around four thousand, most being "advisors" attached to Vietnamese units in the Delta. The Military Assistance Advisory Group (MAAG) and the Military Assistance Command, Vietnam (MACV) had their headquarters in Saigon, and a couple of downtown hotels had been taken over to house military personnel. Still, the numbers were small, and the city was far from overwhelmed, as it was later, by the presence of American soldiers. As a supposed civilian interpreter, I stayed clear of the GI hotels.

Reporting for Duty

The morning after arrival, Tony and I reported for duty at the villa where Mr. Nelson briefed us about our duties. I sensed some uncertainty on his part about what to do with four such inexperienced agents. And I was surprised to learn in this meeting that no one in Central Registry spoke Vietnamese, and, besides me, only Nelson spoke French. For a supposedly covert intelligence-gathering operation in a foreign country, this was very puzzling.

At the end of the briefing, Nelson returned my clothing receipts saying I would not be reimbursed because he himself had not authorized my clothing purchases. Instead, he would assist all of us in spending our clothing allowance. So that evening we went shopping.

Our first stop was the tailor Nankin, whose shop I had already noted in the Passage d'Eden; it was directly across the street from the Continental Palace's dining room. Nelson was already on familiar terms with Nankin and told him our requirements: suits, lightweight trousers, white shirts, etc.—all items I had already purchased and had with me in the hotel. For the four of us, this was a substantial order, and Nankin wielded his tape measure with delight. Next, we proceeded to a shoe store and went through a similar routine. I protested that I did not need more shoes, but the subject was closed. Nelson, as I had anticipated, handled all payments. Happily, as it turned out, his scheme had a positive outcome, for the tailor-made clothes and shoes were of exceptional quality and served me well for long after I returned to America.

My first job at Central Registry was to operate a photographic copy machine located in the darkroom. Working by safelight, the copying was done by a wet-chemical process that involved making a paper negative from the original, adhering it to a sheet of positive photocopy paper, and running it through the light machine. The positive copy was then sloshed in developer, then fixer, then rinsed, and finally hung on a line to dry. It was a slow, messy, evil-smelling, one-sheet-at-a-time procedure done in a hot, claustrophobic, unventilated room. One job I had involved making multiple copies of a fifty-page report; it occupied me all day every day for a couple of weeks.

Don, our photographer, also worked in the darkroom using his own trays of toxic soups. The stifling dead heat and fume-laden atmosphere made us dizzy and gave us headaches. We took occasional fresh-air breaks on the veranda, watchful not to be caught slacking. Much of my darkroom time was spent copying two lengthy documents. One, which was highly classified at the time, contained transcripts of a U.S. Army colonel's conversations with a senior official in the government of South Korea. I wondered why we, in Saigon, were involved in a South Korean political-intelligence investigation; I never found out.

The colonel had long before become friends with a young Korean lieutenant at a military school in the States where they were both students. Years later, when the Korean was attached to his country's embassy in Washington, D.C., and the American officer was stationed at the Pentagon, they renewed their acquaintance. In 1962, the Korean had a cabinet-level job and, unsurprisingly, the colonel was transferred to Seoul, where the two met regularly and had in-depth conversations. After these sessions, the colonel would return to his quarters and record in detail what he had learned. These were the tapes that I transcribed and copied.

I also transcribed and copied the debriefing reports, by Gallagher, of the first American POW of the Viet Cong, a young enlisted soldier named George Fryett. He had been taken captive some months earlier when he wandered by himself beyond the outskirts of Saigon. He was suspected of defection. After months in captivity, the Viet Cong released him, an event widely reported in the American press. Gallagher spent days interviewing Fryett and found that his account of his experience was muddled, sometimes contradictory, and possibly even imaginary. One reader of the debriefing reports thought he recognized details he'd read in a Korean War era pulp novel. The soldier passed a polygraph test, suggesting that he either believed what he was saying or, in his frame of mind, couldn't distinguish fact from fantasy.

Excerpt from a letter to my parents dated May 20, 1962:

My work so far (7:30 a.m.–10:30 p.m.) has been somewhat dull. Much of it has been fairly routine technical stuff running radio and electrical equipment. I have been involved with the security of the top military brass over here.... When I say "top," I speak of no less than four stars. This is interesting. One reason our job is so

Part I

big is that the state of security here is abominable. Compromises of classified documents are frequent, as are "incidents" involving Americans (Army personnel) such as the bomb throwings, and worst of all, loose lipped GIs in bars.

Excerpt from a letter to my parents, June 26, 1962:

> *... Have you read that the VCs finally returned Fryett? That's good. He has lots to tell, as did Quinn & Groom, the two Special Forces sergeants who were captives for 3 weeks. Sure is a shame about the last three who have been killed. One was the son of a major general.*
>
> *It's hard to tell how the war's going. The press over here is worse than at home— very censored and slanted. The way I see it, our only hope lies in the Strategic Village Plan—a long-range strategy to counteract the VC aggression.*
>
> *By the way, have you read "The Quiet American" by Graham Green? It takes place in Saigon.... In fact, the "Continental Palace" even comes into it.*

Eventually, I was promoted from photocopying and released from the noxious darkroom. For a time, I became courier to the American Embassy, which was a twenty-minute drive away in downtown. To show our civilian status, Central Registry had had its jeeps painted black, making them the only black army jeeps in Vietnam—another example of our "deep cover." The embassy run went smoothly and I was assigned the mail run to MAAG, which was in another part of the city. It was a complicated route that wound through a maze of streets crowded with delivery trucks, pedestrians, oxcarts, and pedicabs, but I soon memorized it. This new job not only got me out of the office but along the way I was able to glimpse neighborhoods where ordinary Saigonese lived and worked.

One day, Mr. Gallagher instructed me to take his black sedan because I was to pick up a high-ranking military intelligence officer, who was visiting Saigon from the Philippines, and bring him to Central Registry. I gathered that this individual was Gallagher's boss.

I collected the mail, picked up the officer, and started the return trip. I knew every turn and landmark along the way by heart; however, after five minutes or so, I realized that somehow I had gone astray and did not recognize the familiar landmarks. Nothing looked right. The colonel was in the back seat going through papers in his briefcase. I burst into a panicked sweat. Here I was chauffeuring probably the top-ranking army Intelligence official in Southeast Asia and I was lost in Saigon's maze of twisting streets. In addition, the traffic was unusually heavy with every imaginable vehicle from oxcart to truck, as well as throngs of pedestrians.

I drove on trying to figure out where I had gone wrong, hoping I would soon recognize a building or street corner or any landmark. But

28

no, nothing. I began to feel nauseous. Soon I saw open fields ahead and stopped the car. The colonel looked up from his papers, glanced out the window, and demanded to know where we were and what was going on. I admitted lamely that I had made a wrong turn and said I would turn around and go back and find the right street. In my state, I was not even certain I was accurately retracing the way I had come.

But then, suddenly, I recognized a landmark! It was the place where I had made a wrong turn, and we got back on track. When I pulled up to the Central Registry, Gallagher was outside the gate pacing back and forth; his face was a mask of fury. He ordered me out of the car and got in the driver's seat. Apparently, the colonel was about to miss his flight back to the Philippines. Later, when I was not reprimanded, I realized that the officer had not reported my faux pas: he had covered my butt. A decent guy! Considering the terrible violence, sufferings, and trauma experienced by American soldiers in the Vietnam War, that I vividly remember this inconsequential incident seems wrong; however, in the disciplined hierarchical military culture, that's what happens.

The Case of the
Purloined Penicillin

As weeks passed, I graduated from photocopying and courier service to assignments with somewhat more responsibility, some actually drawing on my training at Fort Holabird. In one of these, our people teamed up with agents from the Criminal Investigation Division (CID) to conduct surveillance of two U.S. soldiers suspected of filching prescription medicines from the commissary to sell on the black market. They were residing in a downtown hotel housing enlisted men. Ordinarily, this would have been a straightforward criminal matter to be handled by the CID; however, in this case, there was a potential security aspect: they were thought to be homosexuals. Back then the military thought gays were susceptible to being blackmailed by adversaries of the United States seeking classified information. (When I was inducted, my medical exam included a brief session with an army psychologist whose only question was, "Are you homosexual?" When I replied in the negative, he sent me on to the hemorrhoids inspection station.) At intelligence school, we were informed that homosexuals in the military socialized secretly and their gatherings were a breeding ground for immoral behavior that potentially led to unpatriotic acts. Even in Washington, D.C., there were "homosexual rings" where gay officers assigned to the Pentagon mixed with enlisted men. Revolving romances, drinking, fraternization, loose talk—all threats to national security. Bring in the CIC. When we flashed our credentials, we struck fear into the hearts of degenerates and spies alike.

In this case, we collaborated with CID agents to bug the suspects' room and monitor their activities from the apartment next door. We worked in teams, one agent monitoring the receiver, one listening at the wall with a stethoscope, and one posted in the lobby with a walkie-talkie ready to follow a suspect if he left the building. It was a monotonous and, to me, ludicrous task, but it was part of Central Registry's raison d'être.

One afternoon during my shift, we were monitoring one of the American soldiers who was meeting with a local fellow. After a while they left the room. In haste, I departed to follow them. Once on the street, they split up, and my cohort signaled he would follow the American. That left me to tail the Asian man, of whom I had caught only a fleeting glimpse before he hopped on a city bus headed for Cholon, Saigon's sprawling Chinese sister city. I hailed a cab and told the astonished driver, "*suivez l'autobus!*" The bus crept along in the rush-hour traffic, stopping every few blocks to unload and take on passengers. Given that cab drivers the world over take pride in the speed and skill with which they negotiate traffic, our snail-pace progress was out of place. At each stop, I would lean my head out the window to see if anyone resembling the subject had exited the bus.

Finally, upon reaching Cholon, a man I thought to be him debussed and headed down a side street. I tipped my cab driver generously and followed. Few Americans went to Cholon, which was considered insecure and unsafe. There was no shortage of Viet Cong and VC sympathizers and collaborators in Saigon; their existence manifested itself in regular bomb-throwing incidents. Cholon was not off-limits, but those who ventured there would not go alone. Their usual destinations were a couple of night spots along the main drag. My man, however, made his way deep into a neighborhood of apartment houses and small businesses. And it was here I found myself, over six feet tall and blond, tailing him. It would be an understatement to say I stood out. What was more, the farther I went, the more I wondered if I could find my way back to the main avenue with the buses and taxis.

Back when I was training at Fort Holabird (only about three months previous), I had participated in two surveillance training exercises in downtown Baltimore and along the city's then-derelict waterfront, where I had dressed disguised as a derelict. In that field training, we operated in teams of three; so tailing a Chinese man in Cholon by myself offered a special challenge. I let my suspect get well ahead, even momentarily out of view when he turned corners. I must say, to my credit—I was not "made," at least by him. It soon became clear, however, that I was not going unnoticed, for I was the most unusual thing to happen in that neighborhood in a long time. It began with a couple of curious children who began tagging along behind me. Then one called out "OK! You number one!" Other kids appeared and walked along with me, chanting, "You number one! You number one!" This, along with "OK," was what Vietnamese bar girls said to GIs when they were treated to a "whiskey." It was the standard phrase to say to Americans. My efforts to shoo the kids away proved ineffective, even counterproductive, as excitement spread and more joined the pack. Finally, when my subject entered an apartment building, I stopped by a newsstand to figure out my next move. What would an experienced counterspy do?

Hollywood movies I had seen came to mind; thus, I bought a newspaper and pretended to read it. It was in Chinese, of course, and after a few moments I noticed I was holding it upside down.

Now the children wanted candy. They ran around, they danced, and they sang out every English phrase they knew. When adult pedestrians began taking notice, I knew the gig was up. I noted the address of the building that my suspect—assuming I had been following the right man—had entered, made my way back to the main avenue, hailed a cab, and returned to Saigon. Now I was a true operative.

Saigon

In Central Registry, I was an enlisted man in the army and assigned tasks appropriate to a novice private. But when I entered the Continental Palace, I became an honored guest. I had two identities and lived in two separate worlds divided by a taxi ride.

On duty days, Tony and I were awakened in the cool early mornings by the houseboy, who delivered our *petit dejeuner* of tea and croissants on a tray. After he drew open the window curtain, I would draw apart the mosquito netting, pull myself out of bed, and sign the chit. On weekends, however, if I wasn't on duty, we would go downstairs and enjoy a quiet civilized breakfast in the dining room. The taxi drive to Central Registry could take nearly half an hour when traffic was heavy, but the fare was only a few cents. The cabs were decrepit Renaults, remnants of French Colonial years. Holes had rusted out in the floors, and various parts were held together by wire. When your cab broke down in traffic, a not infrequent occurrence, you would tip the driver and flag down another one. As a security measure, Tony and I would have the driver drop us off along the main avenue and then walk a few blocks to the villa. There we entered a different reality.

I generally went back to lunch in the hotel or a nearby Chinese restaurant. My regular table looked onto Tu Do's sidewalk, and I would take a chair facing toward the square. Usually, the same waiter was on duty and we soon got on friendly terms. Of course, I should have avoided such a repeated pattern, but people-watching was irresistible, and I grew lax regarding security. From my vantage point I could observe the Saigon girls, with their long black hair, walking by in their flowing *ao dais*, conical hats, and sandals. They were strikingly beautiful but, of course, socially beyond reach. Still, I fantasized scenarios in which I might meet one.

During lunch, the local newsboy would dash across traffic to the sidewalk by my table and sell me a copy of the *Vietnam Times* for ten piasters.

Before I finished, he would show up to buy it back for five. After lunch, I would retreat to my room for siesta and ask the third-floor houseboy—reliably stationed on his mat by the elevator—to knock on my door when it was time to go back to work.

Siesta is a necessity in the tropics. It's a time to escape the oppressive heat and humidity and eclipse the waking world. I would first open the French doors to the balcony to let a breeze waft in. Then I would roll down the mosquito netting, which hung in billowy loops from the bedposts, sprawl naked on the sheets, and allow slumber to roll over me like a wave. Those siesta sleeps were deep and dreamless. When sirens wailed in the outside world, I would hear them as from underwater. Whatever the calamity, it existed somewhere far off. Eventually, the houseboy's raps pulled me reluctantly back to consciousness. Then a cool shower would ready me for the active world and work.

In the early afternoons, the heat intensified, and tension grew in the air as the monsoon gathered energy. When it struck, explosively, its strength was beyond anything I had ever imagined. Violent gusts of wind accompanied cracks of thunder and lightning flashes. Then, in a matter of seconds, the rain lashed down in drenching torrents, and rivers of water ran in the cobbled streets. Cyclos, the ubiquitous bicycle taxis, vanished from sight. People in the streets opened their umbrellas, scurried away from splashing cabs, and sought shelter under doorways, in the Passage d'Eden, anywhere with a roof. I would watch the spectacle from my hotel window or in the shelter of the hotel veranda as I sipped a coffee or *citron pressé*. When I was running errands in an open jeep, of course, I would get soaked. Even though violent and intense, the monsoon storms cleansed and refreshed the city. They injected life and energy and banished any lingering effects of siesta.

I often saw high-ranking American military brass in uniform in the hotel café. It was no secret that a duty trip to Vietnam from elsewhere enhanced one's résumé, which helped when it was time for promotion.

Apparently, these Vietnam junkets by the higher brass grew to be an issue, for one day Gallagher questioned me about the presence of senior American officers at the hotel and told me to try to discreetly find out their identity. This seemed not to be counterintelligence-related but rather a matter of army politics and promotion competition. The next day, I informed him of an air force brigadier general whom I had noted while he was staying in the hotel. Since I had been unable to learn his name, Gallagher asked for a description. I said he was fiftyish, fat, and a

34

heavy drinker, and could reliably be found evenings in the hotel bar. At that point, Gallagher's snappy voice cut me off and warned me to take care how I spoke about officers. So ended that assignment.

Tony and I sometimes made the rounds of Tu Do Street's bars, girls and entertainment being a priority. The ritual was to sit at the counter, order a *ba muoi ba* (a brand of Vietnamese beer labeled "33 Export"), make small talk with the bar girl, order her a "whiskey" (in reality a jigger of tea), and roll dice. The loser, usually the GI, would buy the next round, and the girl would declare, "You number one!" Since the recent passage of a law illegalizing prostitution—promoted by President Diem's influential and controversial sister-in-law, Mme. Nhu—the Saigon bar scene was regulated, and the girls, dressed in uniform-like white *ao dais*, stayed behind the counter and were, as a rule, unavailable after hours.

Letter to my brother and sister-in-law, mid–May 1962:

> *...Things are going OK with me although in certain respects I am disappointed in the setup here. Some of the personalities at work are hard to take, especially the chiefs, who run the office like a POW camp. As far as my own work goes, I'm being "broken in" still. Some of my jobs are very interesting while others are routine. Certainly there is a great deal of variety.*
>
> *I'm residing in the Hotel Palace Continental and have a large room with balcony overlooking the General* [National] *Assembly and center square of Saigon. I often sit out on the sidewalk drinking beer or coffee and watching the girls go by. They're really terrific, and many men-of-the-world have sworn to me, the most beautiful women to be found in all corners of the Earth are in Saigon.... Yesterday, being Saturday, I had some free time and walked through the local food market—never again. Centuries of evolution have given these people strong stomachs, which are hard for Americans to understand. I was amazed* [at some of the foods for sale]— *will tell you details another time.*
>
> *Did you read in the papers about the bomb scares last week? They kept us working long hours, as you can imagine. But these things are infrequent and certainly less of a danger than, for example, simply getting run over by some of the crazy drivers here. Driving is a big free-for-all and a hair-raising experience. Two nights ago I was passing a bar on Tu Do Street when something was thrown by my head into the bar. Everyone hit the floor and scampered, knocking over tables and breaking glasses. It was only a prankster who had tossed a tube of toothpaste, but it shows how edgy people are. The streets and bars and movies, etc., are all closely watched by "sûreté" men.*

Letter to my parents, May 31, 1962:

> *...As I write this, there is a violent thunder and lightning monsoon cloudburst outside. Great fun! Today is Memorial Day—supposedly a holiday. But I worked all yesterday on two important jobs, was on duty all night long, and continued on one of the jobs for eight hours today. ...The Diem regime is staging a city-wide purge to*

Part I

uplift the morals. Last week dancing was banned—ironic, as it's the cleanest thing around and keeps a lot of people out of trouble. Now the dance-hall girls are on the streets, jobless (?). ...I'm going down to a joint to play dice with a beautiful girl who comes from Hanoi and says she likes me. She said it was love at first sight. I beat her in 7 straight games of dice, which is unheard of!

Of course, rules and regulations can be broken. One evening, when I was having a beer at the Continental Palace bar, an attractive young Vietnamese woman came and sat next to me and struck up a conversation. It soon became clear that for a very modest sum she would be glad to come up to my room. Well, she did and stayed all night. This may have been "the Sixties," but in 1962, even at twenty-three, I was as inexperienced in matters of sex as I was in spy craft. To spend the night with a woman—my first time—forged a lasting memory. She wanted to set up an ongoing relationship with me, at her place rather than the hotel, and become my "mistress." Unfortunately, for professional and security reasons, such an arrangement was out of the question.

Letter to my parents, June 19, 1962:

...I am too old to be homesick, but I do, on occasion, think back upon the old time favorite things. Sometimes I think back on Tamar [my girlfriend before being sent overseas], *especially when you talk about Mark* [Tamar's brother]. *If I had not gained wisdom through experience with Lee Sumner* [a previous girlfriend, who dropped me], *I could probably think myself a far-off forlorn lover, and moon at night and so forth. As it is, I realize I have grown up and those days are over. Strangely enough, I have never felt like an adult, as I imagine a 23½ year old is. I always feel like a kid. But being so far away gives me an objectivity, or something—which makes me feel older. Like a few weeks ago I was all bound up in myself and Tamar. Now I don't care to think about the girl* [In fact, I was deeply hurt that she never replied to letters from me], *and I see myself in relation to my work, the Viet Cong, and my boss, and not to a girl, which is so tiresome and involved.*

The bar scene soon wore thin and incentivized me to do other things: walk around downtown, go to a movie, or just stay in the hotel and read a book or write a letter. On my walks, I discovered two Vietnamese nightclubs where you could have a beer without being bothered and listen to female performers softly wail sad Vietnamese ballads. The music initially sounded strange to my ears, but in time I came to like it and appreciate the fact that few Americans went to these places.

Later on, I did make a special friend at a bar located away from Tu Do Street. She spoke French, and our conversations went beyond the regular formula. One afternoon while I was there, she spotted a push-cart vendor in the street and called out an order. The vendor produced a small wrapped-up object, from which she extracted a large duck egg. She cracked it open and removed a slimy unhatched duck. I was shocked—even more so when she ate it with relish and assured me it was delicious and a great delicacy. I declined her offer to buy me one. To my surprise, when I invited her to a movie after her shift, she accepted. We saw *Town Without Pity*, starring Kirk Douglas, a new American film dubbed in Vietnamese with Chinese and French subtitles. Afterward, we took a taxi to her place, where I dropped her off at her apartment. I felt I had had a normal evening and a date with a Vietnamese person.

Major Kumar

One early afternoon, not long after arriving in Saigon, I was awakened from my siesta slumber by knocks on the door. After calling *merci* to the houseboy, the knocking continued. Strange, for it wasn't yet time to go back to the office. I quickly dressed and opened the door, only to find a young woman standing there. She said something in Vietnamese that I didn't understand, so I asked in French what she wanted. Beyond her, down the hallway, a male figure leaned out of a doorway and looked my way. The houseboy, too, was watching intently. I thought I recognized the man and had seen him around the hotel in the uniform of an officer in the Indian army. Now he was in siesta garb: white undershirt and shorts.

The girl repeated what she had said and touched the front of my trousers. Alarms sounded and I shook my head—*Non merci, khong di di.* No thanks, go away. Her offer seemed too blatant, and public. And was she hiding something under her *ao dai*? I had read a few spy novels: in them, approaches by foreign agents were made discreetly, at night, in crowded cafés and smoky night clubs, not in respectable hotels in broad daylight. And so, despite hormonal urges, I returned to bed. Later that afternoon, I thought I should report the incident to Nelson. He queried me about the Indian and told me to photograph the houseboy, which I dutifully did the following day while the fellow was sleeping in the hallway, using the outfit's Minox, a miniature "spy" camera.

One evening soon afterward, as I entered the hotel's veranda for a drink, I saw the Indian officer sitting by himself at a table. He was in street clothes having a *citron pressé* (freshly squeezed lemonade). He glanced my way, showed recognition, and came over to introduce himself. He spoke in a formal manner, said his named was Kumar, Major Kumar, and asked if I would join him for a drink. As soon as I did so, he apologized for the matter involving the woman, for which, he said, he was entirely responsible. The houseboy, it seemed, had let her upstairs, probably for a bribe, and she had knocked first at his door. "I was not interested," he said, "but I suggested she try the young man living at the end of the hallway. Then I saw that you sent her away, as well. Tell me, how can one lie with a woman one doesn't even know?" Kumar shook his head in dismay, and I assured him that I agreed.

Kumar. If I ever knew his first name, it's gone—that memory drawer is empty. In any event, I never used it. We were simply Kumar and Noble, and he pronounced my name like that of the Swedish philanthropist. He looked to be in his early forties, nearly twice my age. Thirty years later, as I write this, I still see him clearly and would recognize him immediately, at least as he appeared then. His complexion was much lighter than that of the fabric salesmen along Tu Do Street, and although his face was quite pockmarked, he was strikingly good-looking. He had thick, neatly combed black hair and was smartly dressed, even when not in uniform. Clearly well educated, he spoke with the clipped intonations of an upper-class, British-schooled Indian. He was shorter than I was by several inches, but he carried himself with a military bearing that lent him greater stature. With me, he was always courteous and sensitive, and I always sensed a genuine warmth beneath his reserved veneer. In short, he liked my company, and I enjoyed his.

During the months of our association, Kumar never imposed himself or assumed I would be free to join him for a meal or walk. "Would you care to join me for dinner this evening?" he might say. Even as friendship grew between us, the formality continued. We often engaged in lengthy talks, but rarely did they lead to personal history or intimate topics. Early in our relationship, he asked what I did. The question was hardly unexpected. I rolled my eyes and replied that I was employed by the army and had a tedious clerical job, though I felt fortunate to be assigned to Saigon and living in this hotel. He seemed to accept the explanation; still, I always wondered what he really thought about my status.

Major Kumar was a senior official in the International Control Commission (ICC), which had been formed in 1954 after the truce negotiations in Geneva that followed the victory of the Viet Minh forces over the French at Dien Bien Phu. That battle, so brilliantly planned and executed by General Giap, drew down the curtain on France's colonial presence in Indochina.

The ICC's mission was to supervise the Geneva Accords. Teams of three inspectors, made up of a Canadian (democracy), a Pole (communism), and an Indian (neutralism), visited military bases in North and

South Vietnam to ascertain that both sides were following the agreements arrived at in the truce. Thus, Major Kumar regularly traveled in both North and South Vietnam. As in Saigon, he kept a permanent room in a hotel in Hanoi, which he used while on official visits or inspections of North Vietnamese military bases. Naturally, I was intrigued by this and very curious to learn about Hanoi and the north.

Typically, when I returned from work at the office, I would shower, change clothes, and go down to the hotel's cafe-bar for a drink. It was my transition from military flunky to respected civilian, resident of Saigon, and honored hotel guest. If Kumar was in town, I would find him at a table along the sidewalk drinking something non-alcoholic—*citron pressé* or tea. He would signal me to join him, and it was clear how pleased he was to have me join him. I would order a drink, we would talk, then we would head off somewhere for dinner. A nearby Chinese restaurant was a favorite of ours for lunch, and a French bistro on a side street off Tu Do, which featured roast squab, but sometimes we ventured farther afield, even to a small quiet Japanese restaurant in Cholon where I would indulge in a flask of sake. Kumar did not drink alcohol.

The café in the Continental Palace was a meeting place for all sorts of people.

At dinner, the conversation usually became more focused. As our friendship deepened, Kumar confided that he was not altogether happy in his job, and sometimes he unloaded his frustrations. As an uninvolved outsider, he found me a good listening post. One frustration he expressed was with the ICC's bureaucracy and its impotence to control the growing militarism in the two Vietnams. Its mandate was to oversee the stipulations of the truce, but he felt he could do little more than observe the disintegration of that truce and submit toothless reports.

Kumar also had some personal problems within his delegation. He was a Hindu, a bachelor, and an upper-echelon officer. The majority of his Indian colleagues, on the other hand, were Sikhs of lower professional rank (and, I gathered, social status) who were married and had their families with them in Saigon. They were a clique, and he made it clear that he had little in common with these people, who were loud, unrefined, poorly

A view of the Saigon River from a promenade near the bottom of Tu Do Street.

educated, and "dark-skinned." He was glad, he said somewhat defensively, that they were not residing in the Continental Palace, so he was spared contact with them after work. Even I had difficulty visualizing Kumar, with his somewhat proper and prudish "English" background, socializing with these burley, warrior-looking turbaned males, and their reticent

Sidewalks along Saigon's main streets, such as Le Loi, were frequently bustling with pedestrians and vendors.

wives. His reference to their dark complexion offered a glimpse into India's caste system, which I had heard about, but little understood. The essence of Kumar's confidences was that his work seemed pointless and he was lonely.

After dinner, we sometimes took a stroll along the waterfront to watch people and small craft and ferries plying the river and passenger ships docked in the port. What territories lay across the river? I wondered. I knew so little about Saigon and its environs. If I hopped a ferry upriver, where would I end up? I had no idea. Probably as a Viet Cong prisoner.

Another favorite stroll of ours was along Le Loi, the wide, crowded commercial boulevard with many shops, businesses, and sidewalk vendors. It led from my hotel to Saigon's vast central marketplace, which was crammed under a single roof and teeming with shoppers. It was filthy, too, and rat-infested. Merchants accosted you—Vietnamese, Chinese, and Indian—and tugged at your sleeves, and waved items from their stalls in your face. It was basic product promotion, but ineffective in my case. Other streets and avenues, wide and tree-lined, reflected the influence of French city planning. The presence of motorcycles, cars, and trucks, on the one hand, and peasants pushing handcarts and driving oxcarts was something I had never seen in major cities in America or Europe.

A farmer and child from the countryside entering Saigon with a loaded cart.

43

Part I

Other evenings, engrossed in conversation, we would perambulate without a plan, exploring new streets and districts. There were tailors and shoemakers, bird salesmen and flower merchants. A favorite shop of mine specialized in variously sized and designed suitcases and steamer trunks fabricated from uncut sheets of Budweiser and Miller beer cans. I've always regretted not having bought one to take home. I remember once asking an octogenarian aunt of mine if she had any regrets in her life. "Yes," she replied without hesitation, "the things I didn't buy."

Now, with Major Kumar, my former lack of concern with international affairs truly began to change; as we talked, my interest in these matters grew and I realized their importance, especially concerning the two Vietnams: Saigon and Hanoi, Diem and Ho Chi Minh, democracy and communism. Up to this time, for want of exposure to any contrary views, I had accepted the prevailing American position: South Vietnam was a struggling democracy threatened by communists; Diem was a good man in need of our help; Ho was the enemy. This was President Kennedy's view and Eisenhower's before. What did I know?

Kumar helped open my eyes and I became aware of my political ignorance, naïveté, and Cold War biases, and I started to view international affairs through his eyes, the eyes of an informed neutralist. He helped me grow up, question things, and think in broader terms. I was no longer indulging in college-campus bull sessions; I was in Saigon, learning from someone experienced in the world, a senior officer, almost a mentor. Without preaching, Kumar gently revealed his views about the world, and it was not a world ideologically divided in two but more subtle, and about people. I began to see Vietnam as a land of peasant farmers caught in a political drama beyond their control. He described the citizens of Hanoi, not as communists, but as ordinary folk, people who, in the early mornings, gathered in the public square in front of his hotel and did exercises in time to music. Also, they revered Ho Chi Minh. These were uncomfortable thoughts that challenged Major Gallagher's caution that whatever we thought, we were not to question our country's involvement in Vietnam. As he had told us, America was committed, and we had a job to do: end of story. It seemed a clear enough directive then, but I began to realize that it wasn't so simple. I was dealing with a house of cards: pull one or two out and the whole structure might collapse. Meeting Kumar was but a first step, for beliefs are not easily abandoned, especially by a young soldier on active duty who was still disinclined to question authority.

Ngo Dinh Diem's regime was fully in power, at least in Saigon. One afternoon, Kumar and I were having tea on the veranda of the Continental Palace when a police van arrived, and the cops began erecting street barricades to divert traffic away from Tu Do Street and the central square. I wondered what was happening. "Probably Diem's motorcade," Kumar said. And sure enough, a convoy of police cars, military vehicles, and motorcycles soon approached down Le Loi and turned up Tu Do in the direction of the presidential palace. At the center was a black limousine with dark tinted windows.

"Look, that must be him," I said.

"Maybe," Kumar said, then explained that for security reasons, the limo's occupant could be Diem's double, with the real motorcade taking a different route altogether. Only members of his personal security guard knew which was which. As the sirens diminished, Kumar told me in his cool, objective tone that he'd recently seen Ho Chi Minh openly give a speech in Hanoi's main public square. Ho was a beloved figure, he said, and was revered as Vietnam's liberator and called "Uncle Ho" by the people. I listened intently.

I decided I should tell Mr. Nelson about my meetings with Major Kumar and requested a meeting. He showed casual interest and directed me to submit a written report about each meeting. In the first one, I told of Ho being cheered by thousands of citizens in Hanoi's central square. As much as this may have been news to me, it hardly was breakthrough military intelligence; still, I thought it might raise an eyebrow or two among Central Registry's desk-bound officers.

One day, after Kumar's return from a week in North Vietnam, he mentioned having inspected a major airbase outside Hanoi. I pricked up my ears and showed interest. He became animated as he described a buildup of Soviet aircraft, and increased numbers of Russian soldiers he had observed on the base. Wondering if he knew who I really was, I expressed only casual interest in what he was telling me. However, the conversation brought into focus a situation: Kumar, my off-duty social friend, was becoming a potential informant. I had thus far steered conversation away from my job, embarrassed by the weak cover story I had been given to account for my presence in Saigon. A French interpreter? Couldn't army Intelligence have come up with something better than that? I told him I was a clerk out in Tan Son Nhut. That sounded marginally better—but a paper-shuffling clerk with a college education living in the Continental Palace? That was a stretch.

I had once asked Gallagher at a staff meeting, "When someone asks me what Central Registry does, what should I say?" He looked bemused and somewhat condescendingly replied, "Say we register centrals and if they ask again, leave the room." Of course, this was ludicrous.

The following morning, I dropped a report into Nelson's in-box about Kumar's observation of the Soviet buildup on a North Vietnamese airbase. Would this catch anyone's attention? It did, for a few minutes later I was summoned to Gallagher's office. The commander was looking at the report and shaking his head. He motioned me to sit down. First, he went into his now-familiar tirade about the incompetence of the agents the army was sending him. Immediately, I regretted having written the report. When his outburst had run its course, he pushed the paper away and turned his small penetrating eyes my way. "Yale," he said with irony, "French literature." I sat still. He threw his eyes at the ceiling, stood up, and began pacing the floor.

"So now I've got a goddamn Ivy League French literature kid fresh out of Fort Holabird handling the potentially most valuable informant in Southeast Asia!" He was shouting now and threw his arms in the air. The adjoining offices had fallen silent. He looked at me and gave a helpless shrug. Then he told me to shut the door.

Gallagher was forty-two, paunchy, short-necked, round-shouldered, with crew-cut steely gray hair and ill-fitting clothes. He looked decidedly unmilitary. His shabby appearance and unpolished manner gave no hint of his being a career soldier—a contrast to Kumar, who was the same rank. In a civilian context, Gallagher might be a shopkeeper or a boxing coach in some gritty inner-city gym. If Kumar was the image of an officer, Gallagher was the stereotypical spy, or counterspy, as was the case.

In counterpoint to his amorphous physical bearing, Gallagher brimmed with energy and intensity, and when he walked into a room, he commanded attention. He had a sharp authoritative voice, alert shifty eyes, and a temper and unpredictability that kept you off guard. He could be sullen, grouchy, and quiet or emotional, even passionate, and verbal. Not infrequently, he would exit his office, stomp by our desks to the patio, and vent his frustrations on the monkey in the tree. "Chico," he would yell. "You're responsible for this goddamn mess!" He had an acerbic wit and a sharp tongue. And he was always impatient. I suspected he had achieved great success in some assignments but was finding Saigon a challenge. Rumor had it that he was long in grade, and I guessed that his temperament had caused further promotion to elude him.

Gallagher returned to his desk and, after perusing my report once more, put it down. He spoke now in a softer tone and said that for a novice like me to chance into a relationship with someone in Kumar's position was—he almost smiled for a moment—unusual. Then he queried me in detail about Kumar. I answered cautiously, sensing a potential predator testing the waters. Could he be considering some type of coercion? Holabird had taught us about that. Kumar was single, lonely, stressed, and frustrated in his job. He never talked about women and had befriended a man half his age. I kept speculations to myself, for I knew that Kumar, even if potentially vulnerable, was a man of honor and dignity. Gallagher must know that any intelligence-collecting adventure involving a greenhorn such as myself and a senior ICC official from a neutralist ally country would carry risk and could have, let's say, unfavorable political repercussions.

In the end, he instructed me to continue playing it as I had been—to keep seeing Kumar and continue showing interest in his trips to North Vietnam, but only casual curiosity. I should gently encourage him to talk but not raise suspicion by plying him with questions; he was to remain an "unwitting informant." Gallagher asked what Kumar knew about me. I said I had told him I was in Central Registry and he had asked what I did there. Gallagher wanted to know what I had replied. "I told him just what you said, sir—that we register centrals." He glared at me, sensing insubordination. I smiled, gaining a touch of confidence now. As a private, I was immune to being busted to a lower rank—there was none. "Actually, sir," I went on, "I told him I maintain personnel records for the army." The commander nodded approval.

As the meeting progressed, I could tell that Gallagher was now seeing me in a new light and allowing the barrier of rank to drop an inch or two. Briefly, he spoke to me as if I were actually a thinking person with a measure of intelligence. I asked what he wanted to know, and he produced a rapid-fire bucket list of desired information about the North Vietnamese air base: types of Soviet aircraft present, identification numbers, how many Russian military personnel, unit insignia, and so forth. Clearly, the Russians interested him more than Ho Chi Minh's popularity. Suddenly, he paused, seeming to become aware of the developing tone of our discussion, and told me to carry on. I exited the room.

And so my interactions with Major Kumar continued as before. We met for drinks on the hotel veranda, took walks, and went out for lunch or dinner. I did learn the types of Soviet aircraft but dared not ask him to describe the insignia on troop uniforms. Enough informational tidbits emerged from our conversations to help offset the waste of my latent talents at the office. Several more times, he inquired about my job, but when I continued to give evasive answers, he dropped the subject. Either he didn't care or preferred not to know. As for me, I enjoyed being the only one at Central Registry with his own "secret agent" in Hanoi. I didn't know it then, but the Kumar business would lead to a new assignment.

Kumar's visits to North Vietnamese military bases were certainly of a sensitive nature, but they were conducted as official ICC business and it occurred to me later that he must have been submitting reports to his own superiors in the International Control Commission. Instead of me trying to glean scraps of information from him on a hotel veranda, why didn't Gallagher or the CIA or the embassy simply request copies from the ICC? They must have been public information.

I seldom socialized with colleagues from the office, other than Tony Brush. Quite apart from the intelligence value of my interactions with Major Kumar, our friendship continued to grow. We were comfortable with each other, shared like sensibilities, and simply enjoyed each other's company.

One day, to my surprise, when Kumar joined me on the hotel veranda, he smiled mischievously and announced there was an American girl he wanted me to meet. She is the daughter of a friend of mine, he said. Without hesitation, I agreed. "And as it happens," he went on, "we are invited to their house on Sunday for afternoon tea, and they are looking forward to meeting you. As is their daughter." I must have looked astonished. "Yes, Noble, it is all arranged, and their house is close by. We can walk there from here." He said the girl was pretty and had only recently arrived in Saigon and was not yet socially acquainted.

Needless to say, I looked forward to this meeting all week long. When Sunday afternoon arrived, I put on my new Nankin suit, and we walked together to Kumar's friend's house, which was on a quiet residential tree-lined street about ten minutes from the Continental Palace. I asked how he'd come to meet this American, and he replied that he was a colonel in the American army, and they were acquainted through work. Now I felt apprehension.

The daughter was as Kumar had described. However, we were both a bit shy and mostly looked at each other while the "grown-up" men made conversation and the mother arranged the tea. Her father, I learned, was with MACV, the Military Assistance Command, Vietnam, the headquarters of General Harkins. He was top military echelon, and, as an enlisted

48

man—Ivy League or not—I knew I was operating out of bounds. Army regulations forbid socializing with officers—fraternizing, it was called—and it would take only a quick phone call for the colonel to learn who I was. But, did the rules extend to officers' daughters? When the colonel eventually asked me what I did, I said simply that I was with Central Registry. An awkward pause followed before the conversation continued on another track.

The next day at work, I reported on the tea party and how Major Kumar was trying to help me expand my social life by introducing me to an American girl. Gallagher called me into his office and forbid any further contact with the girl or her family. As in India, the military's caste system is strict and deeply seated in tradition. There is some irony in this incident because Gallagher had recently called a staff meeting to reprimand us for having relations with Vietnamese bar girls. A fellow agent—Don, who had asked the Pan American flight attendant to watch his valise because it contained secret documents—we learned, had taken a Vietnamese mistress and contracted gonorrhea, which had been reported to his commander. Gallagher's anger at the agent's indiscretion had spilled over to include all of us; we were all guilty in his view. Scanning our faces in moral disgust, he asked rhetorically if there was anyone among us who would bring home a girl we'd met in a bar. No hands went up. The order was clear: local girls were off-limits. In my case, the directive even included a respectable American girl to whom I had been properly introduced over Sunday tea with her parents.

Kumar was puzzled by my reluctance to follow up with his friend's daughter. At my weak excuses, he expressed disappointment, even disapproval, and implied that this was bad form on my part. Eventually, however, he dropped the subject.

Central Registry

Nelson, Hamel, and Gallagher ran Central Registry. As a French speaker, Nelson was able to meet with his Saigon contacts without an interpreter, and he also supervised us agents, even when our jobs amounted to clerical functions. Mr. Hamel, a quiet reserved bureaucrat who was always cordial to his subordinates, seldom left his desk. The organization, it seemed to me, spent an inordinate amount of time managing the constant flow of paperwork generated by the military establishment. We received, for example, regular reports from Vietnamese police and intelligence organizations in Saigon, and these had to be translated, studied, analyzed, and moved in some form up the chain of command. Oh yes, and photocopied.

An original character in Central Registry was Headley, our translator, who had enlisted from the National Security Agency (NSA) and found his way into the CIC. He was a slender scholarly looking fellow with metal-rimmed glasses, and he had a good reading knowledge of Vietnamese, though minimal, if any, conversational ability. Borderline eccentric, he spent his days hunched over the documents he was translating. He had remarkable linguistic ability and was especially drawn to exotic tongues. I gauged his intelligence quota to be somewhere in the high stratosphere. He humored us with witty comments and asides, always said in low tones that were inaudible to the officers. Brilliance did not prevent him from being an enlisted office drudge who seemed never to reduce the stack of papers on his desk that needed to be converted to English. Off-duty, he tended to keep to himself and read books.

Excerpt from a letter to my brother and sister-in-law, July 15, 1962:

... Last night I had dinner with one of the men in my office, the most interesting (to me) and a very friendly chap. He's somewhat of an eccentric and a very unmilitary sort. He majored in anthropology, but his main field is herpetology, his passion being lizards. And he knows all about them, too. This place is a haven of lizards

as they scamper all over the walls. This fellow works for NSA in civilian life and speaks Vietnamese, Gaelic, and some Cambodian and Basque. He likes to be knowledgeable in weird, unusual fields, but he doesn't impose his knowledge on anyone. We walked through an interesting part of Saigon—some streets filled with exotic shops. You see very strange things for sale such as weird fruits and parts of animals and fowl. I saw in one store a platter of roasted duck head and necks, in another, specially prepared baby snakes, in another certain sticks of wood and bark (spices). We looked around a bird store. Parrots sold for 25¢ and other tiny little birds for 4¢ each and 25¢—75¢ for bird cages. Beautiful pots of ivy and tropical plants were being sold along the street as well as an endless assortment of cloth and straw things.

We then went to a Vietnamese nightclub I knew of where girls take turns singing American, French, and Vietnamese songs. These singers are strikingly beautiful, for the most part, and have lovely voices. When they sing VN songs, the sounds are twangy, nasal, and in half-off-key tones ... very good.

Then I went and saw High Society. *Did you ever hear Satchmo speaking French with Vietnamese and Chinese subtitles? It's a riot! But the singing was for real. When the dance scene came, I was surprised to see almost half of the Vietnamese people get up and leave. I don't really understand it all, but it must have been a negative response to the dancing—amazing.*

To alleviate the monotony of his regular translating work, Headley began creating his own strictly private language. Some weeks after I came to Central Registry, a young office clerk from the Midwest named Simmons appeared. With a mop of unkempt black hair and horn-rimmed glasses to correct nearsightedness, he seemed awkward, unmilitary, and unworldly. But he was friendly and vulnerable, and we took to him immediately.

When Gallagher passed by, he would pause with hands on hips and gaze at Simmons, shake his head in mock disbelief, and go on to his office. But Simmons and Headley had adjacent desks and soon developed a close rapport. Simmons was impressed by Headley's unusual qualities and linguistic brilliance. Headley, gratified by the newcomer's unconditional admiration, soon decided he had found the right person with whom to share his invented language. Lessons began. Simmons turned out to be a quick study, and before long the two were communicating with some fluidity. Their cryptic exchanges, however, made Nelson increasingly uncomfortable—his desk was within earshot—and he soon forbid use of the language during work hours.

Another member of the team was Warrant Officer Mike Smith. A career spook with many years of experience, he had taken nearly every technical cloak-and-dagger course offered at Fort Holabird: He could pick locks, open safes, operate various clandestine listening and surveillance devices, and run a polygraph machine. In Saigon, army clerks often forgot or lost the combinations of office safes for which they were responsible, in which cases Smith came to the rescue. Sometimes I accompanied him. Unlike bank robbers in Hollywood films, he didn't press his ear to the mechanism while delicately turning the wheel to hear telltale clicks. Smith was a driller. In his reference book, he would find a diagram of the safe in question, plug in his drill, and start punching holes through the door. Safe manufacturers liked this method.

In addition to the original agents and my group of four, more began arriving. Also, we were served by Wong, the cook; a houseboy; and a laundress, who heated her iron over charcoal. Wong was Chinese Vietnamese, and when the government decreed that Chinese take Vietnamese names, he changed his to Dong.

From my very arrival in Saigon—the airport fiasco and discovery that no one in Central Registry spoke Vietnamese—I questioned the organization's effectiveness. There seemed to exist no depth of knowledge about the country, and as newly arrived agents, we were offered no orientation. I began to wonder what kind of intelligence-gathering operation was going on besides receiving Vietnamese police reports. The United States had never been interested in this former French colony—or in Southeast Asia, for that matter. And how many Vietnamese Americans were there from whom to recruit intelligence agents? In the 1950s, many Asian experts had been purged from the State Department and the military establishment, resulting in a dearth of people with knowledge of and experience in the region. It showed.

In 1962, the Army's principal role in South Vietnam was advisory. Central Registry, on the other hand, operated unilaterally (and supposedly covertly). As low man in an organization in which information was compartmentalized, I was the last in line to know what we did. On the other hand, as the unit's photocopier, I handled a lot of paperwork, including material from Vietnamese military and police agencies and interrogation reports of suspected Viet Cong sympathizers. In many cases, these reports ended with the ominous comment that the suspect died of natural causes after questioning. I would remember this in later months.

As the startup man for a counterintelligence operation, Gallagher must have had an impressive professional background and proven his effectiveness in other situations. He had a tough disciplined work ethic and a no-nonsense, can-do approach to challenging situations. On the other hand, he often showed frustration, and I could see why. His agents had very limited, if any, experience in Southeast Asia; except for one, who had opened a field office in the Delta, no one looked even looked Asian, and some of us were novices fresh out of intelligence school. To me, we looked more like paper pushers than counterintelligence operatives.

On logistics, Gallagher especially deserved credit: he had set everything up—the villa, vehicles, offices and equipment, sleeping quarters, darkroom, and a cook and houseboy. He had also established working relationships with various agencies and set a daily work routine. Everyone looked busy. It was my impression, however, that on the intelligence-gathering front, he was out of his depth, treading murky Asian waters while dealing with the bureaucratic pressures from superiors and the inexperience of subordinates. It must have been a great challenge. To have had our jeeps painted black? Well, that was plain folly. We might as well have painted cloak-and-dagger logos on their doors.

Gallagher was high strung and impatient by nature, sometimes exhibited erratic and irrational behavior, and was prone to fits of anger. When these outbursts occurred, he would sometimes vent his frustration against Chico, the rhesus monkey. The poor beast was less than a picture of health. He leaped around at the end of his chain, chattered, masturbated, and was sexually attracted to the dog. Other times, Gallagher exploded against Wong, who spoke no English. Occasionally, I took meals at the villa and can testify to Wong's culinary competence. On Easter, I remember, Gallagher took exception to the baked ham Wong had prepared, in particular to its being garnished with pineapple rings. This was how baked ham was served in my home, but apparently not his. His anger gathered momentum until he summoned Wong from the kitchen and berated him in front of everyone. The outburst embarrassed all present and was, in my view, behavior unbecoming a senior officer, reminiscent of Captain Queeg in *The Caine Mutiny*.

My guess, in retrospect, is that Major Gallagher, who had spent his professional life in military service, was intensely stressed and frustrated, even in 1962, by the situation he found himself dealing with. Given the terrible consequences of early policy decisions regarding Vietnam and in light of later developments in this long war, it is embarrassing to read what seem like trivial complaints in the following letter.

Excerpt from a letter to my brother and his wife, June 13, 1962:

The big problem here is my commander. He has few human qualities and daily violates every basic principle of leadership. In fact, I actually believe he is going a little wacky. He has frequent temper tantrums during which he loses logic &

Part I

reason. Today he rushed suddenly out of the office, grabbed our watchdog by the throat, threw it to the ground, stepped on it and proceeded to beat it with a club, the whole time cursing abusively. When he came back in, his face was purple and twisted in rage. And he was totally unconcerned, if not unaware, of our reaction to this scene.

He treats us like the dog, only his methods are subtler and slightly less violent. He is the cause of great resentment and discontent among his subordinates, as well as mistrust. In my opinion, although he has a sharp mind in the affairs of his field, he is an incompetent officer. He is the type that in combat gets accidently shot by his own men.

I write my letters in my hotel and keep them on my person until I drop them in the U.S. mailbox inside our office, from whence they are hand carried to the airport by one of our men at 0630 hours every day. The VC have deeply penetrated our installations, but I am pretty safe in saying that these letters get through unread. Mail going through the Vietnamese postal system is often censured and/or read. Nothing I say is of a classified nature.

... I'm hoping to be sent north in a few weeks, and also hoping to get a coastal town with beaches!! Then, too, I could get a bad spot, also. It is my boss's wish to keep us all in suspense, and hold the one dangerous assignment over our heads as a treat. I mean threat!

Helen, would you like a beautiful pair of handmade alligator ($15.00) or snakeskin ($8.00) shoes? Just send me an old shoe & I'll have them made to order. Or a pocketbook. My man will make anything. Hurry though.

Excerpt from a letter to my brother and his wife, July 15, 1962:

... As for taking action against the boss, Helen, it is really out of the question. His "offenses" consist in many minor irritations which build up resentment in his subordinates, but nothing which would serve as significant evidence of any disorder. You have to live with him to see it. When his superiors come around, he is a polite and gentle lamb.

However, a couple of weeks ago, just after George Fryett's press conference, the colonel in charge of the P.I.O. released his name to the U.S. press in connection with Fryett. Gallagher really hit the ceiling, charged down to the Personnel Information Office, and thoroughly chewed out the colonel, who is a superior officer. He had the dumb colonel quaking!

The war drags on here as ever with losses on both sides. The only possible development that I can see would be if the Laotians ever can integrate their forces, organize, and cut off the Viet Cong infiltration routes across the Laotian border. But I don't think this is likely.

Vietnam, as maybe you've read, is having a cyclical rat epidemic, and the government has initiated a big drive to exterminate them. The other day I watched one of the ushers in a most modern theater here chase a large rat all around through the isles during the intermission. He finally caught it and clubbed it to death and carried it out triumphantly. The Central food market (like Les Halles in Paris and Chambers Street in New York) is overrun with the rodents, which are very large and brown.

54

After Don contracted a venereal disease, Gallagher called a meeting and told us that we had too much spare time on our hands and he intended to fix that and improve discipline. To keep us occupied after hours, he created a project—to build an addition to the villa. Nelson divided us into two work crews and developed an after-hours schedule. Under the new regimen, I left regular work at six, took a taxi downtown for a fast meal at the hotel, caught a cab back to the villa, worked till around midnight, went back to the hotel, slept a few hours, and then went back to the office. It was a grueling schedule. I rarely saw Kumar, and when I did, he inquired where I was keeping myself as he missed our dinners and walks together. I explained somewhat lamely that I was working a double shift. So ended my reports on conversations with the "potentially most valuable informant in Southeast Asia."

Another nocturnal job followed the construction work—to conduct a security sweep of MACV headquarters, where General Paul D. Harkins (later succeeded by General William Westmoreland) was commander. This key building, where the high brass had their offices, was a leased building on Pasteur Street near downtown. There was concern that this headquarters might have been bugged by Viet Cong sympathizers on construction crews while they were readying it for use by MACV. We ran technical sweeps in every office and conference room in search of possible concealed listening devices. Was someone eavesdropping General Harkins' meetings? It was our job to find out.

Slowly and methodically, under Smith's guidance, we passed a metal detector over every square inch of the walls. When it beeped, as frequently happened, we would wonder: was it a stud nail, a dropped screw, a scrap of metal lath, or a bug? After digging out uncounted ordinary metal construction objects, we would say, "Sounds like a lost nail to me, let's move on." Tech sweeps are the most boring and tedious tasks in the security business.

If there were listening devices, they would be transmitting. Therefore, we played recorded music in each room we swept and tried to pick it up on a radio receiver. Our reel-to-reel tape had only two songs: Greenfields and Paper Doll. As far as songs go, they were good choices but not to have to listen to continuously, hour after hour, night after night. For weeks afterward, they continued to replay in my head. I wondered if this is how the North Koreans had driven American prisoners to confess. We never found a bug and never picked up a transmission. MACV was clean. The Viet Cong were not the KGB.

Part I

We also tested office security at MAAG, which had a large compound across town. Again, it was a night job. Happily, we did not have to test perimeter security by attempting to penetrate the installation from the outside, a potentially risky exercise. One building we entered had a large central workspace with half a dozen or so desks assigned to office clerks. Half a dozen safes containing classified documents were situated around the room, at one end of which was the captain's office. After rummaging through desk drawers looking for unsecured classified documents, Smith said it was likely that the clerks had not memorized the combinations of their safes but instead wrote the numbers down in out-of-the way places. He told me to find them. I looked under desktop counters and on walls behind file cabinets and other places. As Smith predicted, I found most of the combinations. We opened the safes, pulled out sheaves of documents stamped SECRET and TOP SECRET, spread them out on desktops, and photographed them. We then returned them to the safes and returned to Central Registry's darkroom, where Don made a set of 8x10 inch copies. Before dawn, we had them spread out on the captain's desk accompanied by a note on top giving our phone number and the message, "Call us." An hour or so later, we got the call—the MAAG office was in a frenzy.

Rest and Relaxation
in Hong Kong

On July 1, Central Registry received one R & R (rest and relaxation) pass to Hong Kong, and, on a coin toss, I won it. I had been hoping to use any accumulated leave to visit Phnom Penh. But Cambodia, governed by Prince Sihanouk's supposedly neutralist government, was off-limits for security reasons. So, Hong Kong it was.

Upon arrival at the airport, I took a van with other R & R soldiers into the city and got off at the first hotel drop-off, a small, quiet, inexpensive place about a twenty-minute walk downhill to the harbor. As I stepped off the van, the driver handed me a business card to a tailor named Ah Lee, who, he said, would give me a good deal. That very afternoon, I went to Ah Lee's shop and was measured for shirts, a suit, and a Harris tweed jacket. Almost sixty years later, the jacket, which set me back twenty-five dollars, is still operative and in good shape. As an incentive, Ah Lee offered me and another GI customer who was in the shop a free half-day guided tour of the city in a chauffeur-driven private car. That happened the following morning and included Victoria Peak, Aberdeen, and a medieval-looking hamlet in the New Territories. The driver even took us to the famous Floating Restaurant, where you select the fish you want to eat from a huge aquarium.

I spent many hours wandering the streets, window shopping, people watching, and experiencing the city's many strange sounds, smells, and sights. I even went to a beach to swim and lie in the sun. One night, having read *The World of Suzy Wong*, I explored the Wanchai district on Victoria Island and made the rounds of several rough waterfront bars, which I found patronized mostly by rowdy British sailors on shore leave. Their intoxicated revelry and brawling spilled out into the streets—a far cry from Saigon's tame nightlife. Afterward, I rode the Star Ferry back to Kowloon and hired a rickshaw to my hotel.

Part I

Another evening, I found myself in a bar on Kowloon in the company of other British sailors. One of the chaps became friendly, and we went on together to another club and then another. When we parted company, he invited me to join him and some girls the next morning for a day of sailing. It seemed like an odd offer, but appealing; still, given the late hour and our condition, I doubted it was serious.

Tired and hungover, I nevertheless managed to get up in time, grab some coffee, and make it to the arranged meeting place along the waterfront about ten o'clock the following morning. It was Saturday, and to my surprise my bar friend was there waiting. Before long, the rest of the party—seven of them—arrived and I was introduced to his young English and Chinese friends. They welcomed me to Hong Kong. We strolled together to a nearby yacht club, boarded a sailboat, hoisted sails, and set off. It was a clear, sunny day with gentle breezes. Soon, beer was produced, and as we sailed around Hong Kong Bay, we sang English songs and picnicked. I learned that this disparate group had become friends through a Scottish Folk Dance Club, which was under the auspices of the church they attended.

At the end of our sail, it was dusk, and the girls insisted I view the harbor from a mountain, which they pointed out. So, we squeezed into their car and drove up to a promontory on the mountainside. The lights of Kowloon and Victoria glimmered around the harbor and up the hillsides, and we could make out fishing boats and junks moving around in the bay. To attract fish, the fishermen strung out long nets with floating lanterns, which looked like luminescent pearls on the dark water. Hardly able to bear all this beauty and romance, I decided that Hong Kong must be the best place in the world. Indeed, with its hills and mountains and islands, the city and harbor were like an enormous theatrical set. I kept thinking, what an exciting city this would be to live in, and I wondered how I could come back someday for an extended stay.

Excerpts from a letter to my parents dated July 10, 1962:

I returned from Hong Kong this morning after eight wonderful days in that city of cities. The vacation couldn't have turned out better in almost every way, and I feel like a new man—refreshed, relaxed, and revitalized.

... Then one night I met a young blond Scot in a bar and talked and drank beer with him. He invited me to a beach party on Sunday. What fun! There were five charming Chinese girls of old wealthy Hong Kong families, one English girl named Valery, an Oxford graduate working for the Oxford University Press, the Scot, and myself. The publisher, Hugo, related to royalty, had a boat, and we went to a marvelous beach in his boat and swam all afternoon, me not knowing anyone but soon

becoming fast friends with all. At dusk we returned from the island-beach and drove to the top of a mountain rising out of Hong Kong Bay and overlooking the sea, some fishing villages, and the twinkling lights of many junks. We built a fire of charcoal, and the girls produced a regal feast of chicken and specially prepared beef, as well as sausages, bread, beer, and fruit. We roasted the meat and ate and talked until late into the night. It was a dream. They were all very congenial and happy people, and took me in as one of them although I was a stranger to them all and a foreigner to most of them.

At the end of our day, Valerie invited me to island hop around Hong Kong Bay by ferries the following day, which was Sunday. I met her at the harbor in the morning and we set off. We would take a ferry to an island, hike across, and catch another one on the other side to another island. The rides cost only a few cents each, and she brought a picnic basket.

On one island, a Trappist monk met the ferry and walked us up the path to the monastery and told us the history of the monks, who were refugees from mainland China. Then he set us loose to look around on our own. It was midday in July and very hot outdoors in the sun. We entered the monastery's large stone Romanesque church and sat down to rest in the coolness and quiet. Presently, however, we caught the sound of medieval chanting, which grew louder as a column of monks in hooded brown robes approached and filed into the church. Quickly—we were wearing T-shirts and shorts—we ducked behind a stone pillar. The monks passed by only a few feet away and continued up to the altar, where they knelt in a semicircle and continued their ritual. At that point, Valerie and I became afflicted by an almost uncontrollable case of giggles, so very carefully, hands over mouths, we tiptoed outside, where we drew a deep breath of relief and hurried down the hill to catch another ferry to another island.

Letter to my parents dated July 10, 1962, continued:

The following day Valery and I spent all day exploring various islands and fishing village that she knew of. She acted as guide. Then that night I took her out to dinner and dancing at a nightclub overlooking Hong Kong Harbor, at which time I was the guide. I returned late to my hotel and found that Minni Wei, one of the charming Chinese girls, had been trying to reach me all day. She invited me to her home to a traditional Chinese banquet in honor of Hugo, who was soon leaving for London. She was so disappointed that I had to leave in five more hours. She had a present for me but wouldn't say what it was. The whole thing—her interest, the dinner invitation, the present—was a great compliment to me. I departed sadly at seven the next morning.

Although my week was very good, had I had a second week, it would have been really exciting. I would have gained entrée into some Chinese families, gone to more parties, made more friends, come to know the Chinese, and so forth. These girls

Part I

were aristocratic, some having studied in England and/or Australia, some having been around Europe, all educated and speaking fluent English.

Hong Kong is an extraordinary place, so crowded and full of vitality, so new and strange and exciting, that verbal description would never do it justice.... It thrives on trade and on the sea. Many people live, whole families, in sampans and in junks and gain their livelihood by fishing. The city is built on hillsides and has the same sparkling drama as San Francisco, only more so. Its streets are narrow, steep, and crowded with throngs of buyers and sellers. Weird products and strange foods are bargained for and sold. There is a high tremor of industry and a fervor of life.

During the sailing day, one of the Hong Kong girls had been especially outgoing in befriending me. Before separating we exchanged addresses and vowed to keep in touch. People seldom follow up on such promises, so I was surprised some weeks later to receive a postcard from her saying that she was sailing to Singapore on Messagères Maritimes and her ship would be stopping in Saigon on a certain date. She hoped we could get together.

Excerpt from a letter to my brother and sister-in-law, August 10, 1962:

... Last Sunday and Monday one of the Hong Kong girls stopped by Saigon on her way to Singapore. We had a good time, and I went out to her ship a couple of times.... [It was a] French ship, so I could speak real French with the stewards & officers. From now on I am going to visit these ships when they come into port, as you can buy good beer at the bar and (usually) dance.

A word of explanation about the high-class Chinese girls. The families are very close, very strict and moral. In Hong Kong I would not be able to see the girls alone ... only in a group, and they would be forbidden to date a foreigner. There is a great racial discrimination. Celine [another Chinese girl in the group] explained to me that I would not be able to come to her house and that if I should write, or come to H.K. again, I should write her at the school where she teaches.... The Orient isn't quite as wild and exotic as one imagines. I would say that compared to us, Oriental people have a greater sense of familial discipline and respect. Also they are a more reserved, formal sort, less inclined towards the American spontaneous, easy-going attitude.

PART II

Assignment Pleiku

Back in Saigon, I found Central Registry preparing to relocate from its quiet side-street villa to a much larger house farther out in Tan Son Nhut. What was more, three new agents had arrived and were being quartered in Tony's and my Continental Palace suite. Cots had been installed in the main room, such that our posh private place of refuge had become a kind of barracks. Things were building up, it seemed. Two of these agents revealed themselves to be arrogant career sergeants who talked derisively about Asians. And to me, being of low rank and new to the counterintelligence game, they also were condescending and tried to boss me around. I avoided them and stayed away from the room as much as I could. It was an especially welcome relief now still to have the occasional company of Major Kumar. He had already noticed the increased traffic going into and out of the suite at the end of the hall and thoughtfully conveyed that I would be welcome to share his room, which I had previously noticed had but one large bed. Under different circumstances I might have accepted; in India, for all I knew, it may have been commonplace for two men to share a bed. But since he was a bachelor and never spoke of women, I wondered what he had in mind. We had developed a strong friendship that I didn't want to complicate.

Shortly after, everyone attached to Central Registry moved into our new building, where I was billeted with four others in a small room with no windows and dim lighting. In some respects, I was glad to escape the increasingly disagreeable atmosphere in our Continental Palace suite, even if my new quarters were also cramped. Gone too were the long taxi commutes back and forth to work. Now, in place of the croissant and cold coffee delivered to our hotel room, I was having full American-style breakfasts. There were hot showers, too. On the downside, there was now no escape from the work environment, and, at least for a while, no interesting assignments came my way.

61

Part II

Excerpts from a letter to my parents mailed August 10, 1962:

... I move out of the hotel soon to a new villa in Tan Son Nhut, a suburb of Saigon. There are new arrivals coming in often now and our organization is in a fluctuating and chaotic state. My work is very discouraging ... ever since returning from Hong Kong I've had nothing to do to speak of and so I get the dullest of administrative work. I feel quite useless, which is as demoralizing as the lack of social life and freedom. I look forward more and more to the end of my contract with the army.

... Daddy, I believe Alsop [syndicated newspaper columnist Joseph Alsop] *is 100% correct in saying that we lost in the Laos deal and that the Commies will take over politically. It is easier for the Reds to win a country politically than militarily, and far less expensive. So Laos will fall (I'm certain Washington knew and knows this) and we avoided war. It's tough on the Laotians, but to use the wrong idiom, "C'est la guerre." But with Vietnam it's different.... JFK committed us to the 17th parallel, and we will go to war over that. I don't believe there will be a coalition here, not unless Diem falls and his successor is anti–U.S. That would be sticky. But I expect we learned a lesson in Korea in 1961 and a military (or other) coup here would not be a total surprise on the day of its coming. Who knows what the CIA has up its sleeve?*

A few Australian guerrilla jungle fighters came last week, and even though it was only a token number, it was good to see them and to know that we Americans are not carrying the ball all by ourselves if it comes to a showdown. We're not fighting for Vietnam, we are fighting for California—of course, the Australians realize this in a more realistic way than Europe because they come or go before California.

As you mentioned, the biggest tactical defeat in the Laotian coalition and "peace treaty" is that the "Ho Chi Minh Highway" will become the "Hanoi Super-Throughway." (This is the infiltration area along the Laotian border, in local terminology.) With Castro, we supported a "Democrat" who turned out to be a communist. What should we expect from Souvanna Phouma, a "neutralist" with a communist head of state/brother? I think Alsop is understating the case when he calls it a "poor bargain" or a "weak bet" or whatever, and naïve when he infers that Washington is playing a gamble. JFK decided to lose Laos. It's as simple as that ... just as he has decided not to lose South VN.

In 1962, I believed in the widely accepted "domino effect" first articulated by President Dwight Eisenhower, which held that Southeast Asian countries would fall to the communists like dominoes, one after another, unless stopped by the United States. Vietnam was the immediate case in point with North Vietnamese commies threatening South Vietnam, whose citizens supposedly desired democracy and freedom. Our responsibility was to help the struggling government of Ngo Dinh Diem; it was a worthy cause and I was doing my bit. Even though my friendship with Major Kumar, who was a neutralist and senior officer in the International Control Commission, was expanding my understanding of international affairs, North Vietnam, and Ho Chi Minh, I was still an American soldier.

62

I had sworn an oath, I was on active duty, and I had a job to do. To be sure, questions were arising in my mind, but thus far, they were only questions.
Excerpt from a letter to my brother and sister-in-law, August 10, 1962:

> ... *All is going smoothly here at present. It has been a long time since the last bomb. We were placed on a 4-day alert/restriction over the weekend of the 8th anniversary of the signing of the Geneva Accord, but no excitement. There is always the expectation of an attempted "coup."*

Excerpt from a letter to my parents dated August 12, 1962:

> ... *There is unrest among the natives these days with an expected "coup" in the air. We always expect a revolt, but sometimes it seems more immanent than at other times. The VCs too are fighting with even more vigor and in greater numbers. More often I read in the papers of attacks of 100–200 VC, instead of 20 or 30. This, I do not like the sound of—*

Excerpt from a letter to my brother and sister-in-law dated August 26, 1962:

> *The situation here is darkening. As expected, the VC Army in Laos is moving slowly down here since the "coalition" and we expect a full-fledged military aggression before Christmas. The rains stop in October, the peninsula will dry up by December and then ... (personally, I expect a second Korea) ... time will tell.*

Then one day another new agent arrived at Central Registry. Robert Kuhn was a tall, dark-haired, heavyset man, a seasoned master sergeant about twice my age who had joined up near the end of World War II and spent much of his service time in Germany. Like everyone else except Captain Nelson, he'd never before been to Southeast Asia and he spoke no Vietnamese or French.

One morning, Gallagher summoned Kuhn and me to his office, sat us down, and informed us he had selected the two of us to open a field office up north in a place called Pleiku, a small provincial capital in the Central Highlands, a region inhabited by various mountain tribes. I had heard of these people, the Montagnards. Rumor had it that they were primitive warriors; the Vietnamese referred to them as *moi*, meaning savages. Gallagher instructed us to set up an intelligence-gathering operation there and gave us a short briefing focused mostly on logistics. We would be the first army counterintelligence agents in this region and would be quartered, at least initially, in the MAAG compound on a Vietnamese military base (II Corps headquarters) several miles outside the town of Pleiku. This was just the news I had been eagerly waiting for. Other agents in Central Registry had wanted it. When Gallagher finished, he asked if we had any

63

questions. Kuhn had none, and as the very junior member of the team, I hesitated to speak up. But I did.

"Sir, what exactly do you want us to do up there?"

Gallagher produced his familiar penetrating stare and raised eyebrows, wary of insubordination from this young smart aleck. He turned and gazed out the window where Chico, the monkey, sat in his tree playing with his privates. Then he swiveled around and in an authoritative tone said, "Noble, I want you to collect any information of potential use to General Harkins' efforts in Southeast Asia." I had no follow-up question.

Today, the gnome in my memory pulls a slip of paper from the "Saigon drawer," and on it Gallagher's words are still written in bold. *Collect any information....* The Central Plateau (also known as the Central Highlands), I realized, was terra incognita, at least to army Intelligence. Our mission? Simple. Learn about it. As for "General Harkins' efforts," I was aware they encompassed Thailand as well as Vietnam. Harkins had served in World War II under George Patton, but, it appeared to me, he was now playing war in a region he may only have seen previously on some outdated map, perhaps similar to the one I had found in the Fort Holabird library. As the first army counterintelligence agents to go to this little-known part of the country, Robert Kuhn's and my mission was to find out what we could and tell Saigon.

OK, let's do it.

Excerpt from a letter to my parents, September 2, 1962:

Here it is already September ... two years ago I was beginning my senior year in college at New Haven, and it seems like last year. And last year I was about to join the Army and that seems like a decade ago. Memory is like a camera; instead of focusing depth of field, it plays with one's perception of the passage of time till the distant and far away seem close, the recent long past, and the future mysteriously underexposed. This is especially true with me due to the breach between academic and military life; and especially true with the future as I have news ...In a few days I depart with one other man to a remote jungle region in the mountains of Pleiku Province. There we will set up a regional office and live, presumably, till the end of our tour in Vietnam. So, if I have been operationally inactive during the past several months, this will all change, in fact, already has. We are busily packing equipment and preparing for the move. I will be located outside of the village of Pleiku, living inside of the MAAG compound, safe and sound with American troops all around and the Army of Vietnam close by. You will see on the map that Pleiku is in the mountains so the temperature will be cool and much pleasanter than here in the lowlands. It is about 35 miles from the border of Cambodia, 40 miles from Laos, 80 miles from the seacoast and 380 miles north of Saigon. The country up there is inhabited by aboriginal tribes of fierce mountain people, so lethal and stealthy in their hunting that they send terror even into the hearts of the Viet Cong. Few Vietnamese venture to live in the region as they fear the mountain tribes whom they have never succeeded in subduing and between whom there is a traditional hatred and conflict. We Americans, of course, are trying to win them over to our side as they are invaluable as VC fighters. They hunt with crossbows, arrows, spears and poisoned darts, they run around with nothing on but a loin cloth and they speak a different language (which I am about to begin learning). [This description was based largely on rumors and misconceptions in Saigon.]

The policy of this outfit is that one receives no recognition of the work he turns out (not to mention praise) unless it does not meet the approval of the boss ... then one gets a good "ass chewing." This attitude towards the many hours of work we put in here is often hard to take and certainly gave me the impression that my performance was not outstanding to say the least. I was called in, however, and told bluntly that the Pleiku office was opening, that a linguist (French) and good investigator was needed, that I had been observed to have initiative and not get flustered and that a man was needed who "could really play it cool." I was told that the Old Man had confidence that I could handle the job and that I would be leaving as soon as I could organize and ship the equipment, and "any questions?" My partner is a tough Brooklyn Master Sergeant who, to quote him, "don't take no shit offen nobuddy widdout foist bustin' duh fucken' head uh duh bastard what trows it!" But he is a first rate career man who has been in the organization for seventeen years and really knows the business. If he doesn't know what to do, he busts his way in and finds out. His name is Robert Kuhn.

Among Americans with desk jobs in Saigon, the Montagnards of the Central Highlands had acquired a near mythical reputation. In the excitement of learning about my new assignment in the Central Highlands, I had absorbed and taken to heart the rumors about them. In 1962, there were no U.S. regular troops in Vietnam—they came later—and I had no idea what to expect in Montagnard country, much of which was under the control of the Viet Cong. So my enthusiasm about leaving Saigon and headquarters and taking on a challenge was tempered by some anxiety about being in combat, for which I felt ill prepared.

Excerpts from a letter to my brother and sister-in-law, September 2, 1962:

In certain ways I'm apprehensive since I myself am so new at this business, have never been in combat not to mention even handled a 38 or a 45 which I'll soon be learning. Also, if the VC don't already know I'm coming, they'll find out soon who I am after I get there. As you probably have read, after the formation of the Laotian coalition government, the Viet Cong forces are pouring now into South Vietnam from Laos. Pleiku is pretty much in their path of entry as you will note on the map. Big trouble is awaited before Christmas when these thousands of newly infiltrated troops are expected to stage a major aggressive push, on a larger scale than ever before and with the use of heavier artillery. Many people expect the Vietnamese

defense to buckle and the US to have to come wholly into the war like in Korea.
This all remains to be seen, but it gives me a few butterflies. At any rate I'll be
living in the MAAG compound six kilometers outside of town with good American
and Vietnamese defenses all around.
* ... I've never done anything in the way of arranging for the disposal of my pos-*
sessions in case of death and I feel it's bad luck to make out a will just before
going out on an assignment such as this. So I've made out a witnessed statement
which I'd like you to keep for me till I come home and not to open unless something
should happen to me in the future. Thank you.
* I wrote M&D about this assignment emphasizing sociological interests and cool*
weather, all of which I'm looking forward to. So let's keep the details of the military
situation between ourselves and Daddy. OK?

We flew to Pleiku with our deep-cover black-painted army jeep in
the hold and drove from the airfield to the MAAG compound, which was
located in a corner of the II Corps army base. II Corps was the major military district in South Vietnam's central interior. Initially, we were billeted
with a young Puerto Rican lieutenant in a bare room in the 39th Signal
Corps building. We each had a bunk and small free-standing closet (armoire), and we managed to commandeer a table for our typewriter.

Our space crowded up when a couple of other signal corps officers
moved in. The MAAG commander was Colonel Wilbur "Coal Bin Willie"
Wilson and his superior was Brigadier General Joseph Stillwell, Jr. One
day, General Stillwell showed up to conduct an inspection of MAAG/
Pleiku, which had been newly opened. (He was the son of "Vinegar Joe"
Stillwell of World War II Burma-campaign fame; however, his own career
had stalled, and he was reputedly the longest time-in-grade brigadier in
the army. He was known as "Cider Joe.") When he arrived at our room—
we were standing at attention near the door—he told Colonel Wilson that
it was inappropriate for CIC agents to be sharing quarters with his officers.
Consequently, we were given a new room, which we had all to ourselves.
It was a long, rectangular space that we divided into private and working
sections with a screen.

As we settled in, Rob Kuhn told me that he had been born and raised
in Hell's Kitchen, on Manhattan's west side. His character and personality
had been forged in the rough-and-tumble streets of New York City. He
was tough like a bulldog and even had a slightly jowly look. One of the
entertainments that he and his pals had enjoyed as kids, he said, was to
trap stray cats, stuff kerosene-soaked rags up their butts, strike a match to
them, and set the howling creatures loose in a store crowded with shoppers. He still thought that trick was pretty funny.

With seventeen years in the military under his belt, Kuhn was anticipating retirement. The last thing he had expected was to find himself in
Vietnam—say nothing of the Central Highlands—and he'd already begun
counting the days to the end of his tour. Before coming, he had taken a
short Berlitz course in conversational Vietnamese, actually learning a few
words and phrases, none of which I ever heard him use. His education was
on the job, and I quickly sensed that he had reservations about partnering
with a young French literature major from Yale. Rob was now my immediate superior.

Letter to my parents mailed September 13, 1962:

Dear M & D,

*I came into Pleiku yesterday by plane. It was pretty exciting. Rob and I flew in on
a small aircraft loaded with 3 tons of our equipment including a jeep & trailer. We
sat in the fuselage (?—hull) with a VN WAC* [Vietnamese Women's Army Corps],
*two Americans, an Englishman and a Vietnamese officer. The weather was bad and
we bounced around through the sunlight and monsoon showers. I sported a 38 in
my belt, loaded, and a parachute on my back. Instead of a sexy French stewardess
squeezing a life jacket over her bosom, the pilot barked orders about how to pull
the string to open the parachute once we had counted to three. But, of course, it
was an easy flight and we arrived safely in one and a half hours.*

*The country around Pleiku is lovely. It even reminds me of Dillon, Montana, and
the ranchlands of the far West. The altitude is about 4500 feet above sea level, so it
is very comfortable here now. The days are warm and the nights are cool.*

*We have tons of work to do not the least of which is establishing ourselves and
our office equipment. We have been given a large room by the 39th Signal Bn here
which eventually we will divide into two bedrooms, an office and a living room. But
we do not have the equipment yet, so we are constructing closets out of crates, wir-
ing up our own lights and telephones. There are 4 officers sharing the room with us
but they will be relocated soon.*

*It is about 6 km to Pleiku town ... something less than a western
"one-horse-town" but much more interesting. Before describing Pleiku I guess I
should tell you some background.*

*This mountain country is inhabited not by Vietnamese, but by aboriginal tribes
known commonly as "montagnards" (French for mountain folk). Actually they consist of many tribes of Laotian, Siamese and Polynesian ethnic origin. They are very
small, very dark skinned, and speak their own languages. They wear almost nothing* [Comment: some descriptive comments about Montagnards in this letter are
exaggerated and based on a few first impressions.]; *the men a loincloth, the women
a cloth wrapped around their waist. They have long wild hair and, in all, resemble
the Australian aboriginals if you've seen pictures of them. (If not, look in* Family of
Man *book.) The men have calluses like elephant hide on the cheeks of their rumps
and the young women have beautiful full breasts which sway (or flap) in the breeze.
They give the appearance of a very wild people who know nothing of civilization
and who run about like Adam & Eve before the apple.*

Part II

Ironically, these primitives are playing a crucial role in this 20th century war over here. Although they are at a stone-age level of civilization and hunt with blow guns and crossbows, they will very probably be the main deciding factor in the struggle against the VCs.

I will go into this military aspect a bit later as I will be finding out as much as I can about it. Anyway, these people are what make Pleiku fascinating. They walk through town single file (out of habit from using narrow mountain trails) with baskets strapped to their backs and babies hung on their sides (and usually hanging on to a tit for dear life!). Or they squat around smoking weird pipes, their shaggy hair falling over their shoulders ... an amazing sight!!

A Bahnar tribesman in the village of Plei Mrong, north of Pleiku.

Assignment Pleiku

We eat in the MAAG officers mess across from Captains, Majors and Colonels, which is a change, if not an adjustment. We use the officers' lounge and bar and can see the nightly movie if we want (usually grade C type from the 40s or 50s). When we leave the MAAG compound we always travel together, each with a loaded pistol; but there is little danger between here and town. In fact, it is pretty safe within a radius of 15 miles. We will be traveling a lot, usually by plane or helicopter, but if not, in the company of another armed vehicle. There have been no "incidents" in Pleiku to speak of. The VCs come in and spread around propaganda leaflets occasionally, and one French tea plantation foreman was kidnapped and murdered. But no action has taken place against Americans, and Pleiku is full of security police. Enough said about danger and security; there is really no worry.

A Jarai man and his young son, Plei Bruk Klah, Pleiku Province.

Part II

My French is invaluable here as I am one of the few Americans who can talk with the local officials. As a result of this I foresee that I will become an intermediary between the Vietnamese officials in Pleiku and the Americans. This will be an important job, and hopefully will bring me into the confidence and friendship of the local officials. There is much to be learned if I can get at it in the right way. Robert Kuhn doesn't speak any foreign languages and is a very different sort of a personality from myself. His approach to people is different and it is hard for me to interpret for him.

The French designated this country *Les Plateaux Montagnards du Sud*, the southern plateaus of the mountain people. On its western edge, the mountainous terrain merges topographically with Laos and Cambodia. The French had set this region aside as the domain of the indigenous tribes, a kind of semi-protected reserve that Vietnamese needed a good reason to enter.

Excerpt from an unpublished manuscript I wrote in 1965:

Come early fall in the High Plateau, the skies open up and the planes return like birds flying north after the last cold snap. I used to sit in my jeep on the knoll just south of Pleiku in the late afternoon and look northwards over the hollow wherein is nestled the village. From here I could see the Second Corps Headquarters of the Vietnamese military settled confidently upon a low hill three miles distant. To the west lay the eastern hills of Laos, just below them, Cambodia. I would watch the small olive-drab Army courier plane winging its way across the plateau from Qui Nhon in the last leg of its daily circuit. When a file of Jarai tribespeople was making its sinuous way across one of the fields, baskets on backs, the leader would stop while the others observed solemnly this miracle in the sky. I knew when the plane was carrying high brass up from Saigon on an inspection tour of local headquarters because I would spot a black protocol limousine tearing down the hill from II Corps in the direction of the airstrip. A trail of dust in its wake would drift into the rice.

With the return of the airplanes, the big military operations get back into full swing. The change in weather and firmer ground signal the Viet Cong guerrillas to make for the deeper forests. Several times a week, convoys of trucks pick up columns of troops at dawn outside of II Corps for a deep thrust into the hills. Or the helicopters whirl off to some insecure patch of jungle like a flock of monstrous geese, their bellies pregnant with men. After sunset they return to deposit the weary and the dead.

In late autumn, the tide of battle turns slightly in favor of the national troops and the planes. Almost every day the sky is clear and the sun permits no more than a few skinny wisps of moisture to drift around high up where they cannot even cast a visible shadow on the earth. The plateau lands dry up. The streams shrink to a bare trickle and the earth itself becomes parched and cracked. Vegetation in which one could formerly see growth from day to day withers and the fields turn from lush green to crisp brown. The reddish-brown hue of the soil brightens to a pinkish tan. Even the guerrillas change their camouflage. Finally,

70

so lacking in moisture, the earth powders. The heat and air currents create whirl-winds of dust that spin erratically across the flat expanses. I was always dusty and gritty. If I unknowingly wandered in the path of one of these nose-choking pillars, it would usually miss me, but if not, I would just get dirty quicker. For some of us the dirt seemed to be the main thing about life in Pleiku.

When we arrived in Pleiku, it was still monsoon season and if it wasn't pouring rain, the sky was hazy and the air humid. Rob Kuhn and I constantly had sticky skin and damp clothes. To prevent our shoes from mildewing, we rigged a light bulb in our free-standing closets and kept it on day and night. Outside, we slogged through mud and spun jeep tires in the muck. The rain, warmth, and humidity sapped our energy, and spending so much time indoors had a depressing effect on our spirits. My work downtown took relatively little time during the week, so Rob and I spent long hours in the close quarters of our room with little to do. We soon ran out of things to talk about.

We were the only "civilians" in the MAAG compound. Although everyone knew we were counterintelligence agents, our actual military ranks were classified, maybe even to Colonel Wilson, the top-ranking officer. Given our status (I was a GS-7), we used the officers' lounge and mess. Whatever the officers speculated about our military ranks, they treated us cordially. On the other hand, since the CIC's job (in normal

Montagnard women walking along the road to Pleiku carrying burden baskets.

71

circumstances) involved mostly internal security investigations, there was an undercurrent of reserve and mistrust. Professionally, and even to some degree socially, we were outsiders, and it wasn't easy to make friends. Rob and I had each other for company, of course, but a gulf began to grow between us. This was due mostly to the disparity of rank, age, and experience, but also there was the difference in education and social background. And, as it soon became clear, we had different attitudes and world views. Natural partners we were not, and our relations grew strained, occasionally escalating to overt unpleasantness. Being so inferior to him in rank, I tried hard to avoid arguments or any sort of conflict.

Excerpt from a letter to my parents, October 14, 1962:

> *... Rob and I are outcasts here among the Americans; we do not belong to any unit here, we live by ourselves, but more than that we are by our profession distrusted and avoided. This makes it a bit hard especially as we are ourselves very different in our backgrounds and interests and we live in a single room together.*

Excerpts from a letter to my brother and sister-in-law, September 16, 1962:

> *... As for me, it is hard to go into details, much as I would like to. I have a number of problems. Socially, I have two strikes against me. But this is SOP and nothing new. I live with the US military personnel here in the MAAG compound. My orga-*

The compound of the Military Assistance Advisory Group near Pleiku.

nization is always very unpopular due to lack of knowledge and misconceptions. The military people think that we are here to screw them on security regulations whereas actually we "could care less." In this case my job goes far beyond the ordinary, and this is what will make it interesting. I will be doing a lot of traveling and getting the low-down on certain aspects of the situation here from people whose first-hand knowledge and experience has not yet been exploited.... American and French missionaries, doctors, plantation owners, soldiers, not to mention the Vietnamese types. It is all very challenging. We arrived here last week with a jeep, four suitcases, and four crates, and from that point on the show is ours according to our own ingenuity and imagination. There are two of us. But the problems are many, as I began to say.

... Pretty soon we will have one big room to ourselves. We will get out paintbrushes and plywood and make it shipshape and divide it into living and office space. The weather has been cold and wet so far and I have been freezing, I mean cold. I sent all my warm clothing home. The rainy season ends here in the middle of October. It's funny to think that not far off are elephants, tigers, lions, monkeys and of course Viet Cong. In regards to the last, security measures are strict. Town is off limits to the soldiers after 6:00 p.m., we travel everywhere in pairs and with loaded weapons, and in fact I sleep with a loaded 38 under my pillow (almost). We have to travel around the countryside by plane or in convoys (more than one vehicle), and using the latter method we run the risk of VC taking potshots at us from the woods.

Intelligence Work
in the Highlands

Once settled in, Rob and I went into the town of Pleiku to meet with various Vietnamese officials. Had we not introduced ourselves as counterintelligence agents, my cover as interpreter might finally have assumed some credibility for, initially, at least, I took on the role as Kuhn's translator. Typically, at these meetings, we would appear at an official's office, say hello and shake hands, and, without any preliminary small talk, Rob would launch into questions in his characteristic blunt style. His direct approach, which fell short of courtesy, elicited limited cooperation and, in my view, conveyed an attitude of superiority. I had already sensed that he did not regard these small, slender Asians in high regard and considered them a far cry from the Germans he had worked with before. He seldom remembered their names, and when I reminded him, he mispronounced them. It became clear that Rob Kuhn did not respect the Vietnamese and was put off by having to work with them as equals and colleagues. He was simply out of his element. For that matter, he only tolerated me out of professional necessity. Also, as it soon became evident, he was homesick and missed his wife and daughter.

For me, on the other hand, there were some positives in our new situation. I was free from the drudgery and general lack of respect I had experienced in the Saigon headquarters. But more importantly, I now had an interesting, challenging job with a wide-open goal—to obtain information about the Central Highland region and its people: anything, as Gallagher had said, to assist American efforts in Southeast Asia. Whew. As a teenager, I had gone to school and traveled on my own in Europe, and I enjoyed meeting foreign people and making new friends and learning about different customs and cultures. That came naturally. Also, I found it easy to be relaxed and friendly with the people I met in the Vietnamese army [ARVN], the police, the Sûreté, and the provincial government. As time went on, I made other contacts, too, such as French residents and Christian missionaries. There certainly was nothing to be learned on the II Corps military post, and, whether for business or pleasure, I enjoyed being in the town of Pleiku. Soon, I was given assignments to go other places, both in the Central Highlands and farther away. To do this, I traveled in small planes and helicopters—in a few cases, I drove our jeep—to other parts of Vietnam. And then there were the Montagnards—the Jarai and the Bahnar. I found much to be fascinated by. Some letters, however, reflect a touch of machismo relating to my new role and status. And it took me a while to begin to understand the indigenous people.

Excerpt from a letter to George H. Hobson, dated September 20, 1962:

... Every topic of conversation can lead somewhere when cleverly directed, and every man has certain interests which, when discovered and exploited, will open up his mind and bring you into his confidence.

... This morning I spent with an important Vietnamese "Sûreté" official, this afternoon, with another from a different agency. This evening I talked with a little Djarai tribesman from the back hills. Tomorrow I will go and visit two Evangelist missionaries who serve the aboriginal mountain tribes of the region. Soon, I will visit a fantastic American "guerrier," member of the U.S. Special Forces ... who lives deep in the jungle with Djarai tribesmen. [Note: the term "jungle" is misleading as the country in Pleiku Province was open or forested.] *And there is an American technical representative from a construction company, a high-ranking official from an agency in Washington D.C. and, of course, Army, Air Force and Marine officers and NCOs.*

As the following letter illustrates, after two months in Pleiku, I still entertained idealistic notions regarding the Cold War worldwide competition between Democracy and Communism and believed I was contributing to a worthy patriotic cause. But I had some doubts and reservations, as well.

Excerpt from another letter to George H. Hobson dated November 12, 1962:

I'm "over the hump" on my tour here ... about 5½ months to go unless I'm extended, which is possible. In some ways it is a very good experience, broadening and maturing, but in more ways it is a too limited existence. There is a poor social life, no women, no travel, language barriers, military barriers and only tolerable associates. The work is often interesting, sometimes routine. Certainly I am actively involved in the great struggle between the forces of light and darkness. Communism is beginning to hurt. Helicopters, machine guns, and tactics are beginning to win.

Part II

It's discouraging sometimes to see just what we're fighting for over here. I have little confidence in or respect for the Vietnamese. They are an inferior nationality. The sooner I get away from them, the better as far as I am concerned. I am here to combat Communism, and helping the Vietnamese is only incidental.

Rob Kuhn grew increasingly uncomfortable in the meetings downtown and found it hard to be relaxed and friendly with our Vietnamese colleagues. He became tense and impatient when I conversed with them casually in French. I interpreted for him, of course, but it seemed to frustrate him that his lower-rank partner had an advantage over him. His approach was simple: we were there to ask questions and get answers. Period. After a few meetings, he told me to go ahead and see these people without him. This was a relief for both of us. He stayed in the office, and I was free to operate on my own. I would drive to town, have my meetings, sometimes lunch at a local café, come back, and write up my report. Rob would read and approve it and send it to headquarters in Saigon. This became our standard operating procedure: I did the fieldwork, Rob stayed in our quarters. The arrangement accommodated both our interests and, initially at least, led to a smoother partnership.

On my own, I would typically drop in to see a particular person—a Vietnamese official, for example. Then, after some casual conversation, the official, would initiate our discussion of Intelligence matters, fill me in on what was happening, share his knowledge about the region, and give me copies of Intelligence reports from his organization. This way, the information was being *offered* rather than being *asked for* or, worse, *demanded*. It also meant that we were working together as equals unless, as in some cases, I played the humble petitioner. And, to be clear, I wasn't expecting or receiving state secrets; rather, my contacts were providing routine battle reports, telling me how things were going, and generally educating me. The meetings had an atmosphere of casual conversations, sometimes over tea, and sometimes going out for lunch afterward.

These contacts included an ARVN [Army of the Republic of Vietnam] intelligence officer, the Chief of Sûreté, the Chief of Police, the Deputy Chief of Province, and some other officials. I also regularly met with two missionaries—one English and the other American—who were with the Christian and Missionary Alliance. And, on several occasions, I met with the French manager of the Catecka Tea Plantation, which was located out of town.

Continuation of September 16, 1962, letter to my brother and sister-in-law:

Language barriers are a big setback. I was planning on starting to learn a tribal tongue [Rhadé], *but have discovered that the tribes here are Djarai and Bahnar. I get along OK with any VN officials in French, this being the reason I was sent here. They are terribly nice people, which 98% of the Americans don't appreciate due to the language barrier. In fact, the Vietnamese and I get along better than the Americans and I. The Vietnamese are thrilled that I can talk with them. And it is all pretty high level stuff too.* [Note: In retrospect, by "high-level stuff," I probably meant I was interacting with senior officials. I don't recall collecting high-level intelligence. Through the Freedom of Information Act, I have contacted several army intelligence repositories and the National Archives and requested copies of my intelligence reports; thus far, no results.] *I am saluted admirably by VN majors and treated like an Ambassador.... Little do they know, and I am not about to tell them. But to do what we are supposed to do requires a lot of patience and a lot of sitting around in the beginning. I have a lot of free time now, and boredom is a big threat.*

The Chief of Police was a special case. An officious self-important police captain, he compensated for his diminutive physical stature by wearing a high-fronted police cap and a snappy bright uniform covered with insignias. As a rule, he kept me waiting for ten minutes or so before a subordinate directed me into his office. As I was over six feet tall, he would greet me while remaining seated behind his wide desk. Typically, a corporal would then come in with sheaves of official documents for "*mon capitaine*" to sign. With a well-practiced flourish, the subordinate would spread the papers out on the desk in a broad fan shape, with the first signature line positioned in front of the chief. He would hand his boss a pen and the chief would sign it and pause while the corporal rotated the fan a notch, so the next signature line was in front. And so forth until they were all signed. It was a performance, the intended effect being to demonstrate to this young, tall, slim neophyte foreigner begging information how important and busy the chief was. The ritual done, we would move on to business.

Sometimes when the chief would give me a nice bit information, he would wink and ask if I were sending this directly to the White House. I would respond, "*Oui, Capitaine, directement au président! Pour ses yeux seulement!*" [Yes, captain, directly to the president, for his eyes only.] It became our joke because we both knew most of the stuff he gave me was of limited intelligence value, and probably would wind up in a file somewhere. But it was my joke, too, because he was probably unaware how profound and extensive Americans' ignorance about his country was. Nearly everything was news to us.

Rather than take notes at these meetings, I committed everything to memory. That way, my informants were never quite sure what I was interested in, and this encouraged them to talk more freely. Back at the office—this took some practice as well as twenty-three-year-old brain cells—I would write up what I learned almost verbatim. As for intelligence about Pleiku Province, I took Gallagher's mission statement literally. I ran with the ball, writing reports on a variety of topics until before long they were flowing like a river to Saigon. In my inexperience, I didn't really know the conventions of writing Intelligence reports from the field, and I expressed myself in plain English rather than in stiff military jargon. It was unconventional but made for better reading. Much of what I reported was what I would classify as "general information," probably available in a good French encyclopedia. No matter, I was having an interesting time collecting it. And apparently it must have been of interest to the people in Central Registry and above, for I never got negative feedback. My name was on the reports, Robert Kuhn got credit for being in charge, and Gallagher got credit for being commander. It was a win-win-win situation.

Unless some counterintelligence agents had once worked with Ho Chi Minh against the Japanese in World War II in Vietnam's Central Highlands, I think I was the first army agent ever to operate in Pleiku. At that point, however (late 1962), I was already starting to feel ambivalence about the war and U.S. involvement; still, I was nowhere near turning against it. I felt quite confident I was building a base of knowledge that would help the war effort. Headquarters didn't complain, and they let us alone. Gallagher never came up to Pleiku, nor did Nelson or anyone else from Saigon. As for Rob Kuhn, he never left the MAAG compound. From my standpoint, all this was dandy.

In writing my reports, I was sometimes reminded of reading *Les Lettres Persanes*, an unusual novel of social commentary and satire by Montesquieu I had read in college. The book consists of letters written by an imaginary Persian traveler in France to his wives back home. He describes everything he sees from the fresh objective perspective of a foreigner who understands little of what he's observing. Likewise, I could describe local customs in detail but with only a shallow comprehension of what I was seeing. One thing I was attentive not to do in my reports was to slant things toward what I thought my superiors at headquarters might want to hear. On the other hand, to myself, I sometimes questioned the value of what I was putting on paper, wondering if I should even bother reporting it. My rule of thumb was, when in doubt, write it up. Much later, when I was back in the States, I met someone in the CIC who'd been stationed at Fort Holabird while I was in Pleiku. When we were introduced, he looked surprised and said, "Noble from Pleiku?" I was astonished to learn he had read my reports; apparently, they had become assigned reading at the army's Intelligence center. Well, now Holabird's library had something more than dated love poems to read about Vietnam.

In time, a special friendship developed between the Chief of the Sûreté, Captain Bang (Dại-ný Ng van Bang), and me. The Sûreté was a provincial paramilitary police force. In personality, Bang was quite the opposite of the chief of police; he was an unpretentious, good-natured fellow who immediately put me at ease and clearly took delight in my visits. I'm not sure why we became such friends and can only ascribe it to natural chemistry. Maybe the fact that we, in our separate ways, were both outsiders factored in. Certainly, he had professional politics or stresses to deal with in his job, none of which involved me. So, I was a neutral guy with whom he could relax. Although Bang regularly gave me intelligence, we

Captain Dại-ný Ng van Bang and his children.

79

spent not a little time in his office just having tea and chatting. Sometimes, after our meetings, we went out for lunch or to his home, where I met his attractive, shy wife and their four beautiful young children. A couple of times he even invited me to join him and his family on Sunday picnic outings at nearby Bien Ho Lake, where the kids would paddle around in the shallows and, out of the corner of my eye, I would watch Montagnard women bathing. Rob Kuhn declined to join excursions like this, preferring to stay in the military compound, in our rooms, or in the officers' lounge, where his preferred drink was Chivas Regal, which cost 25 cents a shot. The beer chaser cost a dime.

I also met regularly with a Lieutenant Cuong, an ARVN intelligence officer in Pleiku. One day, he asked me if I would teach English a couple of times a week to him and several other officers and NCOs. This was fine with me. Not only did it provide an opportunity to further develop my relationship with them, but it also gave me an excuse to go into town by myself two evenings a week. I carried my 38 pistol and my carbine.

I started out teaching basic conversational words and phrases, but it soon became clear what these fellows really wanted was military terminology—the terms for various weapons, tanks, equipment, etc.—to help them get a jump-up on being admitted to a U.S. Army school at Fort Bragg, North Carolina, which would enhance their résumé and chances for promotion. This was problematic for me as I knew little army jargon and less about weapons.

Lieutenant Cuong, an Intelligence officer with the Army of the Republic of Vietnam.

80

My ignorance in this matter surprised them, and especially puzzled Cuong. With persistence, he kept trying to find out my salary. At first, I thought he was just curious and wanted to compare my pay to his, but then I realized that he knew something about American army pay scales and was trying to learn my military rank. (He was an Intelligence officer, after all.) I should have found out the pay scale of a first lieutenant and passed that on, but instead I told him that such information was private and confidential. Once you start fibbing, things can get complicated.

Excerpt from a letter to my parents, dated October 14, 1962:

> ... *I teach English to some Vietnamese officers and NCOs in town. This is a lot of fun and rewarding. They are terribly nice men and learn quickly. Sometimes we go out on the town afterwards for some food and drink, which is pretty grim. Vietnamese food is terrible.... I eat it to be polite. They eat all of the beast and do not camouflage it with sharp and somber sauces as do the Mexicans. It is most distasteful and discomposing, and sometimes I suspect it is decomposing too!*
>
> *There's nothing much to report on the military situation here. In my area there has been a slack off of activity, which has various interpretations ... generally the lull before the storm, which is expected before Christmas. The rains are stopping and the days are generally clear and warm. In a month the weather will cool off considerably and the dust will inherit the rain. The earth here is reddish, and when it gets dusty it gets really dirty, as you can imagine.*

One evening after English language class, the guys invited me to take a walk with them in the village. Along the way, they stopped at a street vendor's cart for a snack and ordered some kind of sandwich. When I asked them what they were eating, they grinned. One of them assured me it was a local delicacy and insisted on treating me to one of the same. *Vas-y, mon ami, manges ... je te dirai après*—Go ahead, my friend, eat.... I'll tell you afterward. They all laughed. I did too, as I went along with the gag. When I had a few bites and said it was pretty good, they informed me I had eaten a boiled bull's penis! It was tender and tasty and preferable, I assumed, to the slimy duck embryo that the Saigon bar girl had offered me. I learned of other local delicacies, too: living monkey brains, for example, and a Montagnard stew made of rat fetuses cooked with various roots and herbs.

Although Pleiku was the provincial capital, it was not a large town with, depending on the season, a dusty or muddy main street and several side streets. People gathered at public pumps to draw their water in cans. The main drag had a series of textile shops owned and managed by Indians of dark complexions. Indians were Vietnam's ubiquitous street merchants. There were other shops, too, including a jewelry store where I considered investing in a gold wedding ring for potential future use because the price seemed remarkably low. Not knowing how to evaluate gold, I squeezed it between my fingers and, to my dismay, it folded in. Assuming this signaled poor quality, I forewent the purchase; later I learned this signaled high karat content. I also frequented a photography studio whose owner processed my pictures.

Pleiku had two deputy province chiefs, one a Vietnamese (and a Buddhist) and the other a Jarai Montagnard. I had only a nodding acquaintance with the Jarai, whose main role was to be liaison between the provincial government and his people. However, I met regularly with the other deputy, who, not being part of the Roman Catholic political clique, was a real outsider in government circles. He was ever friendly and cordial when we had tea and chatted, but he kept his cards close to the chest, and I initially learned little of meaningful intelligence value, especially as regards the political scene.

When I showed up at one meeting, he had another visitor, whom he introduced as Mr. Ton That Dinh. Major General Ton That Dinh (Tôn Thất Đính) was the II Corps commander. A flamboyant martinet who sported a swagger stick, he was sometimes a butt of jokes among the U.S.

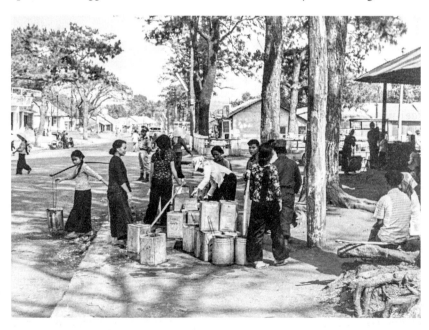

Townsfolk in Pleiku drawing water at a public well.

82

personnel. (Such humor was misguided, however, for he later participated in a coup against the Ngo Dinh Diem regime.) I was puzzled to be meeting a man with the same name as the general, and I assumed that the deputy was joking. When the gentleman and I shook hands, I said, "Pleased to meet you, but don't you think one Ton That Dinh is enough?" An awkward silence ensued before the deputy politely informed me that this was the general's brother. What was more, there were other brothers, all with the same name, except that, in each case, "Dinh" had a different tonal mark. Some lessons are learned the hard way.

While in Pleiku, I made the acquaintance of the manager of the French-owned Catecka Tea Plantation, which was about twenty kilometers outside of town. By this time, although nearly everyone I had dealings with knew I was some sort of spook, I still used a cover story, when necessary, about what I was doing in Vietnam. The plantation manager, Claude Salvaire, had the courtesy not to ask such questions. He clearly enjoyed talking with an American who spoke his language. After spending many years in Vietnam, little must have surprised him regarding what people really did, regardless of what they told him.

Claude invited me to visit him and promised gin and tonics as an incentive. I took a daily quinine pill as a prophylactic against malaria but thought his method of administering the remedy preferable. Given my mission in Vietnam, I regarded Claude as a potential informant and did, in fact, produce several reports containing information gleaned from our conversations. Admittedly, however, they were opportunistic spin-offs from what became an enjoyable social acquaintance and chance for me to see another dimension of life in Vietnam.

When Claude and I bumped into each other in town, we would have coffee or lunch at the French-Chinese restaurant. I made several Sunday-afternoon trips to Catecka with Marco Einaudi and others. It was about a half-hour drive on a rough road through country we referred to as "insecure." In my jeep or Marco's Land Rover, we drove as fast as the road permitted, one of us at the wheel, the other riding shotgun. I remember feeling a rush of adrenaline as we sped over the landscape. On one trip, we stopped to check out the site of a recent U.S. plane crash in the tea fields.

Claude showed us around the plantation, with its extensive tea fields and large processing plant, where women sorted large basketry trays of black tea. His claim to have the largest tea plantation in the country and second largest in the world may have been exaggerated; on the other hand, it was, indeed, vast, and one of his main clients was Lipton.

Workers processing tea at the Catecka Tea Plantation.

Seeing how tea was grown, dried, and processed was interesting, but our objective was the veranda of Claude's spacious house. There, under the influence of gin and tonics, he regaled us with stories, his favorites being about his tiger hunts on the property. Trophies on the wall bore evidence of his shooting skill. His hunting method, he told us, was to tie a live goat to a tree out in tiger territory and wait in a blind through the night. When he heard the sounds of a tiger killing the goat, he would shoot it, presumably under a full moon for illumination. On one occasion—I suspect a gin-induced tale—he dispatched two tigers with a single shot, the bullet passing through the nearest and into the heart of its mate, who was standing behind. I later learned that during the political turmoil and near anarchy of Vietnam between the fall of Dien Bien Phu and the rise of Diem, roving bands of private militia had decimated the population of this beautiful wild animal in the Highlands. And Claude, sadly, had played his part in the slaughter.

In the wisdom of long hindsight, I realize such trips involved a bit of youthful bravado and thrill-seeking foolishness. I've since read, in fact, that over the course of the Vietnam War, more Americans were taken

84

captive by the Viet Cong in the countryside around Pleiku than anywhere else. But at that age, I thought myself invulnerable, especially with my carbine and .38 pistol.

Excerpt from a letter to my parents dated November 23, 1962:

Enclosed is a picture of me looking over an L-19 reconnaissance plane which crashed near Pleiku on October 26th (natural causes). It is lying in the middle of a field of tea on the Catecka Tea Plantation. I'm sporting my .38 and carbine.

Well, tomorrow is Thanksgiving. Sarah Bell [my first cousin] writes me that there's a big family gathering in the offing in Groton ... sounds like fun. I'll be thinking of you all. I received a fine letter from her—she sounded as if she'd grown up quite a lot since a year ago. She wrote me that Aunt Helen used to pray for me over here.

For the past 3 weeks I've been quite busy. I'm working on a very important case here. If we crack it, it should be about the biggest thing in Vietnam and involves a communist espionage net in at least five neighboring countries.

... I dare say the war is going better. Just this week we shot 3 communist tribesmen outside of town thanks to a reliable intelligence report. Six months ago this simply didn't happen. And last week to the east of Pleiku the commies burned two villages, burned 90% of a year's rice harvest and kidnapped 212 villagers (Tribespeople). This then is the method which they are being forced to use in order to gain the support of the common people ... all good signs. Now, it's just a question of time.

The author, standing next to a U.S. plane that crashed in the Catecka tea fields.

Part II

One of Claude's stories I fully believed involved an incident that occurred before I arrived in Pleiku. The Strategic Hamlet Program had gotten under way, and President Diem was scheduled to come to Pleiku specially to tour a new Bahnar defensive village located close to town. There were many preparations to be made before his arrival in order that everything looked shipshape and exemplary.

The afternoon before the president's plane landed, a contingent of police arrived at Catecka. The captain declared that they had come to take the plantation's fruit orchard, which they needed in connection with Diem's forthcoming visit. Since Claude's operation existed at the pleasure of the Vietnamese authorities, he had no option but to comply, and he agreed to the financial compensation offered. The trees were then sawed off at their base, tossed in trucks, and transported to the Bahnar hamlet. That night, postholes were dug, and the tree trunks inserted such that when Diem's limousine passed by the Bahnar defensive village, he would have further visual evidence of the program's success and prosperity.

My report on this incident pointed to the political sham and corruption underlying South Vietnam's war effort and how the as-yet unrealized failure of strategic hamlets could be made to look successful to the upper echelons of political leadership. The incident made me wonder, on the American side, what exaggerations or misrepresentations were being generated by the army for the benefit of Defense Secretary Robert McNamara and President John Kennedy.

Dope, Drink and Sex

The Montagnards smoked fat, dark stogies that allegedly would give you a buzz. What was more, the leaves could be purchased at Pleiku's open marketplace at the edge of town. For security reasons, we had been advised to stay away from there. But, in view of Gallagher's directive to collect "any information" that might be helpful to the American effort, I decided to go shopping. One evening, I drove to the market, which was a poorly lit, spooky place at night, left my jeep on a side street, found the vendor of the leaves, and bought a small bagful for a few piasters. The stuff was black and pitchy, and even though this *was* the sixties, I shied away from sampling it. What I did do was send it to headquarters with a short report. Although the information seemed well outside counterintelligence interests, I thought the report might give the folks in Saigon some entertainment. To my surprise, I later learned, they had sent it to the FBI lab in the States for analysis, and the test results came out "positive"—it was, indeed, some kind of dope.

I frequented the Blue Spring Bar in Pleiku where, as in Saigon, two or three local girls would invite us to buy them shots of their colored-water beverage while we drank *ba muoi ba*, chatted with them, and tossed dice. One evening, a new girl—she spoke French—showed up from Saigon, and we enjoyed having conversations. She stayed only a couple of weeks, but before going back home, she gave me her address in Saigon and invited me to call on her. On a later trip back to headquarters, I did just that. My cyclo driver found her house, and when I knocked on the door, it was opened by an older man—her father. He seemed surprised to find a tall blonde American standing expectantly before him. But he was cordial and spoke French and invited me in. He told me with pride he had served in the French army. Although it was mid-afternoon, he said his daughter was sleeping. He offered me tea and we chatted until she appeared. Courtesy and small talk helped overcome the awkwardness of the situation.

Part II

However, there was someone else who turned up at Pleiku's Blue Spring Bar— a fun-loving, free-spirited young woman who spoke French and liked to party. On numerous occasions we had a beer or two together and talked, and she let me know that for a certain monetary consideration, she would be willing to have me stay the night with her at her house. There was one problem, however: security. A curfew. Staying in town overnight was verboten. Even when Rob Kuhn was away, it was out of the question for me to park our black army jeep on

A bargirl in Pleiku's Blue Spring Bar.

The author and friend in the Blue Spring Bar.

a street through the night. So, rendezvousing with this woman was some-thing I could only imagine.

But then fortune smiled. Kuhn went to Saigon for a few days, and a friend, Marco Ein-audi, who was in an-other branch of military Intelligence and kept a small rental apartment in Pleiku, asked me to look after his Land Rover while he was out of town. I really liked that vehicle, in which we sometimes took Montagnard kids for

88

spins around the countryside. Use it all you like, he said. And I did, first inviting Bang and his family to go to nearby Bien Ho Lake to picnic and swim.

Interestingly, the woman in question was much attracted to Marco, who was tall and handsome with curly black hair. Rumor had it—or maybe Marco admitted—that she'd offered him her services gratis. He, however, was devoted to a girl back home. He regularly recorded and sent off cassette-tape messages to her, to which she reciprocated. (The following year I attended their wedding.) Marco was a Harvard graduate whose father was a professor at Cornell and whose grandfather had been the first premier of the Italian Republic.

Now, with Kuhn gone and the Land Rover in hand, I made plans to visit the woman a few nights later. But a couple of days later, when I appeared at her door, it was an elderly woman who answered. She said she was my friend's grandmother. Oh no, I thought. But she welcomed me into the front room and then, my luck holding, she vanished through a door and in her place my date appeared. She was more than I imagined—hospitable, easy to talk with, experienced, and tolerant of the pent-up energy I released repeatedly through the night. After a final pre-dawn

Marco Einaudi driving Montagnard children around in his Land Rover.

89

tryst, I contentedly drove back to the post. I was twenty-three and finally learning the ropes.

One day, Rob Kuhn announced he wanted to throw a party for our Vietnamese contacts in our quarters at MAAG. Of course, they were very pleased by the invitation. However, Rob had his own idea of hospitality— he wanted to serve them martinis. I told him that they drank little alcohol and not hard liquor; as for martinis, even many Americans find them unpalatable. I suggested wine or American beer. But no, he was determined—martinis it would be, to be served in water glasses. When they came, my colleagues were hard-pressed to hide their distaste for this bitter cocktail, but out of courtesy they took a few sips. Rob made up for their small consumption.

On another occasion—again, Kuhn was absent—Lieutenant Cuong and Captain Bang invited me to dine with them at the restaurant in the village where I often had lunch; the food—French or Chinese—was passable and the water reputedly safe; it was the best eating establishment in town, at least for non–Vietnamese. (The toilet facility, however, consisted of a barnyard outhouse in the back abounding in flies.) Bang had brought with him an attractive young Vietnamese woman recently arrived in town from Saigon. After my hosts ordered bottles of champagne, the party got rambunctious. I had grown proud of my ability to wield chopsticks and remember stupidly trying to lift my stemmed champagne glass with them. Disaster. When the party ended, Bang told me he'd brought the woman for me—apparently, she was seeking a mutually convenient arrangement with an American—and he wanted me to take advantage of his gesture of friendship.

Today, more than half a century later, when I look back at that proto version of myself, I'm astonished (though forgiving) at some of the behavior I exhibited. Oh, to be twenty-four again! No, perhaps not. In this instance, for starters, I had stayed in town too late and drunk too much. Consequently, I landed on the dumb idea, one that only hormones and champagne could inspire, to bring the young woman back to our quarters at MAAG. I shouldn't have been behind a wheel, to say nothing of trying to smuggle a woman into the II Corps military reservation in an open jeep. Crazy, yes, but also a challenge. As we sped out of town and across the countryside, the cool night wind in my face brought me somewhat to my senses, and I pondered how to pull this off, or whether to go back. The post's entrance was guarded by a pair of ARVN sentries with submachine guns. Stubbornly, I dismissed the option of taking my new friend back to town; I was committed to the adventure. And besides, to turn around and go back meant losing face, both to her and to Bang. I did have some pride. As I approached the guard station, I slowed down and motioned the woman to crouch on the floor. Then as we arrived, I stepped on the gas and drove through the gates fast enough that the sentries barely had time to return my salute. Thankfully, they didn't fire or summon the military police. It was done.

We shared my single cot for the night, during much of which, to my surprise, she listened to a Vietnamese opera on my transistor radio. I awoke in the morning with a throbbing hangover. It was hot, the sun was blazing, and everyone was about; in fact, I heard troops marching along the road outside. What was more, Kuhn was due back anytime. The only thing to do was do it and act confident. The two of us got in the jeep and drove down the main II Corps thoroughfare, past the ARVN head-quarters building and alongside ranks of marching Vietnamese soldiers, some of whom cast curious sidelong glances at my companion, whose pink-flowered *ao dai* was fluttering in the wind. I dropped her off in town and that was that.

The Montagnards

As a rule, I worked on weekdays and had weekends free. Sometimes I drove our jeep out to one of the nearby hamlets, especially Plei Bruk Klah, whose inhabitants were of the Bahnar tribe. An army pal, an American master sergeant, often came along with me. As soon as we entered the village, people would gather around us, especially children. We would talk with them and hand out treats to the kids and I would take photographs—portraits of the people and pictures of their houses. Occasionally, we would find the people beating on drums and brass gongs, dancing, and drinking rice wine. They always invited us to partake of the wine and sometimes to join them dancing, as well. There was a studio photographer in Pleiku—he specialized in wedding portraits—with whom I had developed a friendly working relationship. He developed my films, made small prints, and, to demonstrate his skills, insisted one day on making several Hollywood-style portraits of me. The next time I was at Plei Bruk Klah, I would hand out photos to the people. For many, it was the first time they had seen pictures of themselves, and they could scarcely hide their delight. Color films I sent home for my mother to have processed. My missionary friends Charlie Long and Victor Oliver were avid photographers and had their own darkroom setup. They enjoyed showing me their pictures, and it was when I first saw their portraits of the tribespeople that I realized that photography had the potential to be more than snapshots.

Letter to my parents dated October 14, 1962:

It is a very slack Sunday afternoon and I have been reading some English short stories. I was supposed to go and visit the Catecka Tea Plantation which is located about 20 kms. north of here, but the other people decided not to go and I was left without escort. It is the largest tea plantation in Vietnam, I think, and supposed to be very interesting. I'll get there another time.

Several days ago I visited a Djarai village with two other Americans. What an experience! The man who took us there is an old friend of these Montagnards as he has been going out there now for several months and often helps them sell

A Bahnar mother and her children at their home in Plei Bruk Klah.

crossbows to the Americans. They all adore him ... he is an enormous fat man of the jolly variety, and just the type to make a smashing hit with aborigines. So when we got to within a few hundred yards of the village gate, a gang of children swarmed about the jeep. My friend, Walter Long scooped up one and plunked him down in the jeep and introduced him as Sam. I think it was Sam's first ride in a vehicle and he was too thrilled for words. Later on Long called over another whom he had helped cure when he had been very sick as a baby. This too was Sam; it turned out he called all the boys Sam and all the girls Mabel. They are really cute children; that is, they are like any children throughout the world except they are little shaggy, brown-skinned creatures who run around the jungle without a stitch of clothing. [Note: this description, as some of my photographs testify, was exaggerated, apparently for effect; Plei Bruk Klah was located in open country, not in a jungle, and only the youngest kids went around without clothes.]

Charlie Long, an American; Victor Oliver, an Englishman; and a third missionary were associated with the Christian and Missionary Alliance and lived in a compound in town. They regularly went out to distant Montagnard villages to preach and try to gain converts. Charlie also gave Sunday morning services in the enlisted lounge in the MAAG compound, sometimes assisted by a Jarai lay minister he had converted and trained. At one service I attended, this tribal man gave the sermon in the Jarai

93

A Bahnar man with children, Plei Bruk Klah.

language while Charlie translated into English. Charlie taught me a lot about the indigenous people of the Highlands. He knew I lived at MAAG and must have been aware that I was an Intelligence agent. But, being strongly anti-communist (a missionary colleague and friend of his in Ban Me Thuot was being held captive of the Viet Cong), he was willing to share information and educate me a little about the Jarai with whom he worked. As to intelligence, I was mostly collecting information about people, culture, and customs. However, given Major Gallagher's broad mission statement, it was useful and well received. Most American soldiers being sent to South Vietnam knew little to nothing about the country, so the more we understood about the tribal groups, who controlled two thirds of the land mass, the more effective we could be in fighting the communists. That was my working theory, at least. Who actually read my reports? Beyond a few people in the Saigon office, I had no idea. Whatever their fate, I found the research I was doing to be tremendously stimulating and broadening of my horizons. Also, in the process, I was discovering that I had an interest in anthropology, a subject I hadn't studied in college and knew little about.

One thing of which I became convinced: the Montagnards were being exploited by both sides in what I increasingly viewed as more of a civil war than an invasion from the north. ARVN soldiers would enter through their hamlets by day and take food and scold the people for cooperating with the Viet Cong; later, after dark, the Viet Cong would show up, take what they needed, propagandize the village, recruit support, and punish those who had cooperated with government forces.

South Vietnam's government—this was supposedly the brainstorm of Ngo Dinh Nhu, President Diem's brother, but was inspired by prior British policy in Malaysia—had devised a new plan, which was to force rural village folk to leave their homes and rice fields, relocate to "safe" areas, and build "strategic hamlets." These were fortified villages surrounded by palisades and moats full of sharpened bamboo spikes. The hamlets were closed off at night to hinder entry by the Viet Cong. In this way, the government hoped to gain control of rural areas and tribal territory, where the Viet Cong were thriving. The United States supported the strategy by sending over our most elite soldiers—Special Forces, known as Green Berets—to train the Montagnards in self-defense.

Excerpt from a letter to my sister and brother-in-law, October 5, 1962:

I have been in Vietnam for five months now and I am only just beginning to really understand what is going on. I spent a week traveling in the field and around a city called Phan Thiet, which is on the coast below Nha Trang. It was a very interesting experience for me and instructive, too. I got out in the countryside and saw the peasants working in their paddies and the little children riding their water buffaloes. The Asians are so different from us. Sometimes they are disgustingly dirty, sometimes they have a resigned dignity in the face of hardship, which is very admirable.... The [Montagnard women] placidly walk down the main street of Pleiku in single file behind a man, wearing hardly any clothing, barefoot in filth, with a heavy pack on their back and a baby slung around their side.... The child's "security blanket" is his mother's breast, and he gets it continually on the run while she is at work. Girls, women and old women stagger under incredible loads as a matter of course. I saw an army truck (VN) sideswipe a woman riding her bicycle

95

A hamlet's defensive moat with its sharpened bamboo stakes to keep out the Viet Cong.

with a big load of firewood and send her sprawling cut and bruised over the gravel. The truck driver stopped, screamed angrily at her for getting in his way, and then drove away without helping her. Throughout, she sat sullenly by the road, showing no emotion whatsoever, asking no sympathy and getting none. She must have been boiling inside, as I understand that these are passionate people, but she gave no sign of it.... This is how they are. I am sure that after such treatment by Vietnamese soldiers, she and her children will henceforth be communist sympathizers.

It is also amazing to see Americans and aborigines living side by side. We eat three hearty meals a day, live in private bedrooms with fans and G.E. refrigerators, listen to transoceanic radios, and so on, and they, a hundred yards away, sit on a mud floor, live in straw huts, eat a ball of soggy rice with the rain dripping down on their leprosy sores. One has to understand the thing historically and sociologically and culturally to accept it as the natural course of things. We have worked centuries to gain what we have, and they have lived equally as long without developing.... As it is, some of us give them a little help and a few of us devote our entire lives to serving their physical and spiritual needs (missionaries). Someone immature in his thinking could easily be thrown off and shocked by the contrast. One American woman here, horrified that babies of these tribespeople did not wear diapers, distributed some around, only to be more shocked by seeing the fathers happily snatch them off their babies' bottoms and put them proudly on their heads for hats. Even more funny than seeing some Americans trying to deal with ... [Montagnard] culture is seeing them try and deal with 20th century U.S. things. One Djarai tribesman was seen trying to drink a Coke out of a Coke can.... He was trying to suck it through the seams without opening the can. They cannot express their awe at a big U.S. helicopter roaring a few feet over their remote jungle huts.

Thank you for your good letter, Essie. I have been wondering how the little guy is [her newborn son, Stephen] *but of course not worrying as you can handle anything along those lines. Don't take my comments about Vietnamese and Montagnard handling of babies to heart. They have iron immunities, which we have lost, and the ones that run around are the ones that have passed the test of survival ... many do not. I wish I could see you as a new mother; however, when I return, you won't be such an old one.*

I should be getting home in May if all goes according to plan. If there is a big change in the military situation, I might return at a different time. Some people expect a major VC push before Christmas, however, I am becoming a bit skeptical about this as I am in the zone where the buildup is supposed to be going on and there is not that much evidence to cause a panic. It is terribly hard to tell how many VC there are and how many are infiltrating. ...I was in Saigon the other day and was told by the chief that I am doing a good job at this assignment. Thank heavens for the experiences I have had in the past in dealing with different sorts of people and for my French, as both are indispensable here. The work I am doing is quite important. I think this is the first time I have done anything important other than for myself. Sometimes it is very challenging. I got in a tight spot just the other day and have my fingers crossed now that it doesn't make the headlines. But we learn by mistakes and if I don't get caught in this one I'll be in good shape. [Note: My mistake was that I had talked too candidly with an American reporter and feared he might quote me in a forthcoming article. To my relief, he didn't.]

A word of explanation regarding my descriptions of the indigenous people: I had been brought up in a quite sheltered Anglo-Saxon, Protestant academic community in New England, attended private schools and college, and had little exposure to racial and ethnic groups of people as different from mine as South Vietnam's mountain tribes. When I observed them walking to Pleiku barefoot and carrying heavy burden baskets on their back with a tumpline across their forehead, I saw them as poor, backward, uneducated, uncivilized, and primitive, and even wondered if they were a lower order of humans. At the same time, however, they intrigued me. I wanted to learn about these people and wished I could communicate with them. So my mind was full of contradictions and I was in a steep learning curve. To the Vietnamese, the tribal people *were* inferior; they were *moi* (savages) and the Vietnamese treated them badly. Although I, too, initially viewed them as inferior to Westerners, I sided with them because I was struck by their poverty and how they were being exploited. Not to mention they were our allies against the Viet Cong—or so I believed at the time. In a word, I was confused and unsure what to think. As time went on, however, my attitude began to shift and preconceptions and biases slid away. Photography influenced my thinking about Montagnards. Through the viewfinder of my camera I came to appreciate the grace and dignity of these native people, the beauty of their homes and family relationships, and the natural harmony of their way of life.

After returning to the States, my sister, Sandra, introduced me to an anthropologist friend of hers at the Smithsonian Institution, a linguist who had worked with tribal people in a different part of the world. We had dinner together and afterward he asked me to tell him about the

A Bahnar woman at Plei Bruk Klah.

Montagnards. When I referred to them as "primitive," he stopped me and asked what I meant. I elaborated—no shoes, hardly any clothes, spears and crossbows, animists, and so forth. He said it sounded like I was assessing the superiority or inferiority of people based on who had more or less things. People and culture, he explained, were more than having stuff.

Also from the September 16, 1962, a letter to my brother and his wife:

> *Howdy from the high plateau region of Vietnam! That's where I am now, believe it or not. I'm in a little one-water-buffalo town called Pleiku where there are two hundred or so US troops stationed in the role of advisors to the VN Army units here. It's a pretty fantastic place in certain ways and in other ways just a crossroads in the middle of nowhere. Let's start by describing the good side.*
>
> *Pleiku is in the heart of S.E. Asia, which in itself is interesting .... The inhabitants of this region are weird little folk called "montagnards" by the French, and the name stuck. Actually they are very primitive people of Laotian and Polynesian stock who for centuries have lived up in these highlands in separate tribes, isolated from the progress of civilization and the influence of governments. They stand somewhere between Frenchmen and Pygmies, have dark, leathery skin, wide eyes and big feet. They wear nothing but a tattered jock (loin cloth) or, in the case of women, a ragged cloth around the waist.... In all truth, they are wild people who run around naked, with long hair, carrying baskets, babies, crossbows and blow guns. They walk single file due to the narrow mountain trails and when they come into town they still walk single file just out of habit. Many have never seen*

A Montagnard walking along the road south of Pleiku.

99

the face of white men, not to mention machine guns and helicopters. [Note: Given the long French colonization of Vietnam, this was inaccurate. It's also evident that I enjoyed describing the Montagnards to my friends and family as "primitive" and "wild," an urge I got over with time.] *All of a sudden they are caught up in the focus of the world, the battles between the forces of Light and Darkness, and the poor souls simply don't know what in hell is coming off.* [Note: This, too, I later learned, was factually untrue.] *They are playing a really vital role, militarily, whereas, in fact, all they care about is growing their little rice patch and playing it safe with whomever comes hell-raising into their hamlets. It's a 20th century tragedy. In one case, one single village was burnt down by first the Viet Cong (because they'd heard some of the local people had been helping the Vietnamese) and soon after by the VN forces (because they'd heard the opposite). However, the VC treat them worse as they depend upon them for food. The "montagnards" can hardly support themselves, not to mention the VC to boot. By tradition, they hate the Vietnamese, but of recent, the VC have proven to be the greater evil. The result is that the VN government is beginning to bring the mountain people down out of the highlands and resettle them in the valleys in VN controlled territory. If this works, it will be a very severe blow to the Viet Cong forces and a very important issue in the war. This is, as you can imagine, a subject in which I am trying to do some research.*

Children in Plei Bruk Klah wearing clothes collected and sent by my mother.

Disturbed by how impoverished the Montagnards were, I asked my mother to organize a collection of clothing in the school community where we lived in Massachusetts. She enthusiastically embraced the request, and before long cartons of used clothes began to arrive. Initially, I handed clothes out to people in the nearby hamlet of Plei Bruk Klah, but then I gave the cartons to Charlie Long, who passed them out in more remote villages where he went to preach the gospel. Like all young girls, the Montagnard girls loved dressing up in the exotic clothes and I took many photographs of them and the boys to show my mother and her friends. Looking back, however, I suspect most of the children looked upon the clothes donations as a fun costume party and did not continue to wear them in their daily lives. Still, I'm sure the cloth did not go to waste.

Excerpts from a letter to my parents dated October 28, 1962:

I certainly have been appreciating getting the N.Y. Times, and catching up on the news. It makes a big difference....

Well, things really look grim in Cuba! I am very fearful of a war, but can't believe it would really happen. I'm certainly glad that the free world is behind us.

Thanks, D, for the good article on SVN [South Vietnam]. *I thought it was well informed. In a war like this it is very hard to see the forest for the trees, even for me. However, if the communists continue their basic current military methods, I can see only a gradual improvement. We are becoming more aggressive, and if the "strategic village" and resettlement programs are effective, the VC will continue to hurt logistically. Red China has its problems and doesn't seem about to throw itself behind Hanoi, a resort which Ho Chi Minh would*

Two Bahnar girls wearing their new American dresses.

Part II

only turn to in desperation. We are pushing the strategy of training and indoctrinating the tribesmen. And it seems now as if Diem is more willing to go along with this. It's sort of like Chiang Kai-shek asking a Mississippi segregationist to cooperate with colored people against the Yanks! "Who the —— is that Chinaman to tell us how to treat our niggers?!" The VN bigotry and racism against these mountain people is disgraceful....

Enclosed for you are some pictures I took of tribespeople in a village near here. By the way, if there is an

A Bahnar man of Plei Bruk Klah who especially enjoyed being photographed. The author would have prints of the hamlet's habitants made up and hand them out on his next visit.

available source of old clothing in the neighborhood or Groton School, it would be a very good charity to send some over. Maybe you could put a notice on the school bulletin board and include a couple of appropriate photos, and the boys could get together and send over clothing they don't need. Especially, little clothes for the children and babies ... sweaters, shirts, clothing material (no shoes). This is just an idea for your consideration. It would also help me to gain the confidence of the people. They do need the clothing; even old blankets from which they could make clothes. Besides being a good charity, it would help the U.S. effort over here since the attitude of the Montagnards is a vital issue. It would be for the Djarai tribe, people who

A Bahnar woman at Plei Bruk Klah.

102

The Montagnards

have been moved from their traditional homes and rice fields to gov't resettlement villages ("strategic" type) and who are having a tough go of it right now. Last week, the VC burned 157 houses of these people just south of here, leaving hundreds cold and destitute. If you should collect any clothing, have it mailed (surface) to me and I'll distribute.

I'm going on a 3-day trip tomorrow. Will visit Qui Nhon, Nha Trang, Tuy Hoa, Ban Me Thuot and Duc Me. Should be interesting.

Excerpt from a letter to my parents dated November 23, 1962:

I just got your letter, M, and would like to answer it now even though I just sent you both a letter. Your Thanksgiving greeting arrived the day after my Thanksgiving but on yours, so it was almost like having two Thanksgivings!

That's great news about the clothing that you have all sent. Please thank the Congletons and Hardcastles and Wrights for me. You mentioned before in a letter that the [Montagnards] in my photos had clothes on ... look again ... clothes? Mostly, the men only wear a loin cloth although some of the ones who have been around town have picked up regular clothes. Some have French army clothing, and I often wonder how they got hold of it: i.e., what happened to the French soldier who was wearing it. The women wear either just a skirt, or a dress depending on the weather. The villages which are safe for me to go to are the least needy, so I will probably just bring a few handfuls to them and give the rest to my missionary friends who are in touch with some of the poorer people or who can give it to tribespeople who have been made destitute by the communists. These people are

A street scene in Pleiku showing vendors, a Montagnard with his woven burden basket, and off-duty Vietnamese soldiers.

103

very good with their hands and can make terrific things out of the barest essentials. I have bought a few of their musical instruments and weapons which I hope to find some way of getting home next year. They make guitars, violins, flutes, crossbows, sabres, knives, spears, baskets and straw rugs. In their own element they make us look like less than amateurs. I asked a Special Forces major how they were at picking up our guerrilla training. He laughed and replied that they were teaching us how to fight in the jungles, and we were only issuing weapons, organizing them and getting them on the right side. They are fabulous fighters, know the jungles like the back of their hand, and above all know where the VC are. They can walk all day and night non-stop through rough country in their bare feet where the ordinary Vietnamese or American's strength would fail. So, in their own [element], they are not to be underestimated. But this is off the subject of cloth-sewing. I'm certain they can sew although I have never seen one doing it. I have only a distant association with them due to the language barrier and the insecurity of the places where they live. The longer I am here, the more chance there is that the communists know about me and will lay for me if I give them the chance. So I don't stick my neck out. I play it safe and always go well armed. A few weeks ago, the VC tossed a bomb into our villa in Saigon. Luckily, it was a bad shot, so no one was hurt and not much damage was done. I have no indication that the VC know my identity or my mission here; however, if I were picked up in some Montagnard village in civilian clothes, I would rate a fast free trip to Hanoi or Peking. Pleiku and the surrounding area is quite secure. There have never been any incidents around town involving Americans, and in the area, only occasional shootings by snipers. The reason for

A Montagnard home near Pleiku. Note the building's locally gathered materials, the stacked firewood, the pig and piglets, the woman and child on the front porch, and the nearby storage hut.

this is that Pleiku is swarming with military and security and paramilitary forces. An example is the [provincial] fair, which has been going on now for 3 weeks. The VC threatened openly to create incidents at the fair. But security is so tight that they haven't had the chance. There is one part of town which is a bit insecure not to mention unsanitary. I've never been in that section myself, but I know that the Americans who do go there have not run into any trouble (except VD type). Saigon is a bigger target for the VC than Pleiku and I really feel safer here than there. I am very safe as long as I am sensible.

Excerpt from an article by me, "The Mountain Tribes of Viet-Nam" published in the New York City weekly newspaper, *Manhattan East*, November 2, 1967:

When I used to fly over the Montagnard villages, I was struck by the sight—rare in America—of their being laid out according to an orderly plan. Their thatched huts are built on stilts off the ground, a style of architecture affording numerous advantages—snakes are kept out of the bedroom; inhabitants keep dry in the rainy season; shelter is provided for firewood and for the chickens, goats, pigs and cows that make up every household. A notched log serves as a ladder up to the narrow porch and entrance. Inside, the family lives all together. It is the custom for a

A platoon of Montagnard spearmen marching in Pleiku.

Montagnard crossbowmen on parade in downtown Pleiku.

A platoon of barefoot Montagnard riflewomen marching on Independence Day. Ton That Dinh, the commanding general of II Corps, is visible in a white uniform and cap on the reviewing stand.

106

new husband to move into the home of his wife. As the family grows, so does the house. Since for parents, future security rests in their children, unlucky is the couple who has only sons.

The Montagnards speak monosyllabic languages in which many concepts taken for granted by civilized people find no expression. Having no clocks or calendars, they sometimes described when an event occurred by indicating the height of their rice at the time. Some Americans were astonished to find out that the tribespeople did not keep track of their age, at least by calendar years.

I was surprised to see women doing heavy physical labor. It is common to see a column of women walking single file along a footpath with seeming staggering loads of firewood on their backs. They bear many children but many of these do not live to enjoy childhood. The last baby is always on its mother's breast while the one prior to it is carried around on the hip of an older sister. The little boys, meanwhile, run and play and practice shooting their toy crossbows.

On one of South Vietnam's national holidays, provincial officials organized commemorative events and a parade that especially honored the Montagnard paramilitary auxiliaries. An archway on the road entering town read *Mừng Ngày Quốc Khánh*, Happy Independence Day. Everyone in town, it seemed, turned out to attend the ceremonies. Rank after rank of barefoot Montagnard warriors marched down the main street dressed in their native clothing and carrying spears and crossbows. They were followed by a rifle platoon of Jarai women marching barefoot in their native hand-woven black-striped skirts and shirts, their hair well-oiled and neatly pulled back. They looked marvelous and shone with pride and grinned openly at the applause from the onlookers.

Pleiku's Missionaries

Charlie Long and his missionary partner, Victor Oliver, preached the Gospel to remote Jarai and Bahnar settlements. They always welcomed me when I stopped by their residence and they always made time to have a chat and show me their recent photographs. My visits with Charlie, however, began to incorporate what for me was "business": picking his mind for information that might be useful to military intelligence, or simply to further my understanding of the indigenous people whom he was trying to convert to Christianity.

Excerpt from a letter to my parents dated November 23, 1962:

The missionaries in town are American Protestants. There are three, actually one is English. They work out of the Christian and Missionary Alliance in NYC. They are evangelists who have a very fundamentalist point of view in their beliefs with a strong sense of sin, the devil, and literal interpretations. One of them, Charlie Long, who lives over here with his wife and two children, is returning to the States soon after me. He will spend a year on tour giving lectures and conferences about his work over here. I think he would be a valuable speaker to get at Groton School. [My father was on the faculty of this Episcopal boarding school.] *He is 28, comes from S.C. and is very congenial. I cannot imagine anyone who could be more instructive to the boys concerning the dynamic and down-to-earth work of the Christian Church and concerning the other fascinating aspects of their work here ... political, sociological. He is an amateur photographer and has some terrific pictures. I plan to write to Mr. Crocker about this so that if the School is interested in getting him it will put in an early bid and arrange it financially with him. I know that one purpose of his return is to raise money for his missionary work. Before joining the CMA he was a Presbyterian; he joined CMA because of the opportunity to do missionary work which this organization offered. Next week I am going up to Kontum (60 kms north) which is the center of the Catholic missionary effort in the High Plateau.* [Charlie Long recommended that I meet and talk with a missionary doctor in Kontum.]

One time, when I stopped by the missionaries' compound, Charlie was running his weekly leprosy clinic in the front yard. Six or eight

Montagnards were waiting their turn to have him needle-prick the tips of their fingers and toes to test for numbness, a symptom of the disease.

Another time, when I visited, in the late afternoon, I found him much agitated because a Jarai woman he knew had appeared at his doorstep with a set of newborn premature twins, one of whom was beginning to have trouble breathing. The mother had come to him from the local hospital after the staff there had ignored her. Charlie's wife was away, and he didn't know what to do and asked for my opinion and help. These were the first newborn babies I had ever seen. I was astonished by how tiny they were and, of course, I had no experience or wise insights to offer; just the sight of them intimidated me. The twin with the breathing problem was turning blue.

Charlie and his wife had two children and he remembered that somewhere in the house they had a how-to baby book by Dr. Spock. He found it, and frantically we thumbed through its pages until we came to the chapter explaining how to treat a baby having difficulty breathing; it advised extracting mucus from the throat with a suction bulb. Charlie found one and, sure enough, when we inserted the nozzle in the baby's throat and sucked, we noticed improvement. Spock emphasized the importance of keeping newborns warm and gave pointers on how to make a home incubator. We found an old orange crate, lined it with towels, and rigged up a low-wattage lightbulb inside to provide heat. I made a soft nest of rags on the bottom and deposited the babies inside. Each one just fit in my hand. Their exhausted mother watched us anxiously.

With the babies settled in, we relaxed, but not for long because when we next checked on them, the same little fellow was choking again. This time the bulb was less effective, and we could see him losing ground. In this case, Spock recommended applying mouth-to-mouth resuscitation. As I think back, that was some book. Charlie asked me to do it, but when I leaned over and put my mouth on the baby's, I clutched—I couldn't bring myself to blow into that tiny mouth for fear I would injure the boy. I had never even done this procedure to an adult. So Charlie did it and it seemed to help, at least temporarily.

More from the October 28, 1962, letter to my parents:

A few nights ago I was having dinner at the home of some missionaries in Pleiku. That morning the missionary's Djarai pastor's wife had twin sons, born prematurely at 7 months. They had visited the mother and children in the Vietnamese hospital here and found that the babies were not being cared for. They weren't even being kept warm. So the missionary decided to bring them to his home and care for them. We built a little incubator out of a crate, heated it with light bulbs according to directions of Dr. Spock (they had a book on Baby Care) and put the babies inside ... they were only 15 hours old, and tiny, tiny little creatures. Djarai are small people and these were premature twins. (Incidentally, they were covered with black hair—head, faces, back, legs, arms, etc.)

About 10:30 one began to fail. The span between life and death in a 15 hour old baby is pretty small. It couldn't breathe and its lungs had stopped. We kept it alive for an hour and a half through artificial respiration (mouth to mouth & moving its legs) occasionally pulling congestion out of its throat. Twice we thought it was dead as its extremities turned black and its face purple. But by blowing in its lungs we kept its heart going.

At midnight we decided to take it to a doctor 6 kms. away along a terrible road through the country. I tore ahead alone in my jeep, got to MAAG and woke up the Doc. Then minutes later my friends arrived with the baby. They had given it mouth to mouth along the whole trip and, just before arriving at MAAG, it had started breathing again on its own. We discovered that the "Doc" was not a real doctor, but only an Army Officer authorized to dispense pills. He had no oxygen and couldn't help. But the baby had regained its normal coloring & was breathing and we decided it best to bring it back to its "incubator."

Later on in the night it died. We really struggled, but the odds were against us. I think all the artificial respiration drained its little strength or ruptured an internal organ. Last I heard its brother was well and thriving. Baby death rate over here is very high due to lack of medicine.

In the morning, Charlie was philosophical about the incident, pointing out that the woman still had one healthy baby, and Jarai mothers with twins usually favored one over the other until the weaker one died. He pointed out that in this country death was not a tragedy, it was an everyday reality. Weak infants have

Charlie and A. G. Long of the Christian and Missionary Alliance outside their home in Pleiku.

no place in the Montagnard world. Still, I thought, basic medical attention might have saved the baby's life.

In Montagnard society, illnesses and injuries were normally treated by a shaman, or "witch doctor," as we called them. When a Jarai acquaintance of Charlie's told him that a man in his village was suffering from a serious foot wound, Charlie asked me to help transport him to the Vietnamese army hospital, where, he thought, the man had a better chance of receiving medical attention than at the public hospital. When we arrived at the fellow's hut, I saw that his foot and ankle were badly swollen and black with gangrene. This was very serious. We helped him into my jeep and drove him to the hospital in Pleiku. But unfortunately, it was Sunday and no doctors were on duty. We found an attendant, however, who registered the patient and found him a bed in a ward. He assured us that a doctor would treat him the following morning. The Jarai man must have found the hospital environment too strange and too scary to endure, for when I returned on Monday afternoon to see how he was doing, I learned that during the night he had vanished. In Montagnard society, medicine, like religion—the two being inseparable—is deeply entrenched in cultural tradition. To apply Western medical practices to a tribal person requires sensitivity, understanding, and patience, principally to assure the patient that he or she is safe and can be helped.

Another time when I stopped by to see Charlie for my regular Intelligence chat, I found another man with him, an American who had just flown in from Da Nang, a city on the coast. Charlie invited me to join them for a cup of tea and the three of us sat in his living room for about twenty minutes awkwardly making small talk. Soon we visitors realized we were both spooks who had turned up on the same kind of business. Since the other man had come from farther away—I guessed he was a CIA agent—I decided the polite thing to do was to excuse myself and leave. I did wonder, however, how his questions would differ from mine. Charlie seemed quietly amused by the situation. Later, I advised him to have his spies queue up at the door, first come, first served!

More from my September 16, 1962, letter to my brother and sister-in-law:

> *The other day I went in town and met three Evangelist missionaries, two of whom have been preaching the Gospel to these primitives for the past four years. It seems to me that the Montagnard people have enough problems without hearing about the sins of man and God's forgiveness, when they have never even heard of God. But the missionaries are filled with "the Word," speak the languages of*

the tribes, travel around through dangerous country in their truck by themselves, unarmed, and know a lot about the situation with the tribal people. So they are important to me. Today I went to church and sat through an incredible sermon about the blood of Christ, the sins of man, and seven unchallengeable "proofs" of the divinity of Christ. I don't mean to sound sacrilegious, but this was strictly "holy roller" stuff which is bad enough in America and really quite meaningless to the Asian mind. They preach the fundamentalist line where values are black and white and where one is a "believer" or an "unbeliever," the Bible is the ultimate historical authority, and the passion of Christ is described in vivid, dramatic and emotional ranting and ravings. I only go into this because religion greatly interests me, and the idea of westerners preaching such concepts to aboriginal tribesmen in the mountains of S.E. Asia in the middle of a vicious war seems to me preposterous and totally unrealistic. However, I admire the dedication, courage and selflessness of the three men. They also go into leprosy-ridden areas and treat lepers, risking their own health. It is a very noble effort.

Excerpt from a letter to George H. Hobson dated May 14, 1971:

I do hope you did not take that remark about Charlie Long in a challenging way. I did not say it out of ignorance of theoretical Christian faith but rather out of some understanding of Christianity in practice. Charlie was not grievously mistaken in terms of his own faith; on the contrary, it was strong and gave convincing form to his own life.

What was upsetting was that his own experience in religion did not give him any respect for the sacred lives of other human beings. He was some sort of spiritual imperialist, tramping roughshod over the sacred and holy ground of those whom he considered his religious inferiors. It is an attitude which is very common among Americans in foreign lands which they do not understand, common also among the more fervently evangelistic Christians, especially Protestant, which is essential to missionaries. Missionaries usually pick poor "primitive" folk to go among, where they can swing their cultural and worldly weight to great effect. Charlie Long, among his ignorant tribesmen, gave Christianity (Christ) credit for everything from penicillin to the atom bomb. And he managed in his way to save a few souls. He brought in one of his saved souls to preach at a G.I. service and I was so embarrassed I had to leave—like a southern gentleman, of days gone by, bringing Amos out of the kitchen to sing Negro spirituals for the invited company.

The history of Christianity in this country—among Native Americans, that is—is much the same. The missionaries were the vanguard of the Army and afterwards they went about picking up the pieces.

Travels Beyond Pleiku

A basic responsibility of the CIC is to carry out investigations of military personnel who need a security clearance—they are rated confidential, secret, top secret—and I sometimes traveled beyond Pleiku to conduct interviews for this purpose. These trips took me to the provinces of Kontum, Dak Lak, Gia Lai, and Binh Dinh and provided me opportunities to see and experience other parts of the country. Apart from security-clearance interviews, my general mission always was to learn all I could about the country and the people. This was the most interesting aspect of my work. The trips had another benefit that became increasingly important—they gave Rob Kuhn and me some welcome separation.

Kontum

Charlie Long knew I was trying to learn all I could about the Montagnards and suggested I go to Kontum, thirty miles north of Pleiku, to meet an American doctor who had a medical clinic and hospital there. Her name was Pat Smith and she had started her practice several years before. Since military transport to Kontum was not available, I drove our jeep. The road went through a region where the Viet Cong were active; they even had their own Montagnard training camp somewhere in the forest in that area, though we did not know exactly where it was located. Due to the risks, I was anxious about driving to Kontum by myself. I carried a sidearm, drove fast, and felt my adrenaline pumping.

Kontum was a smaller town than Pleiku and I easily found Dr. Smith's hospital. She was in her thirties and greeted me cordially and showed me around. It was a small hospital and all the beds in the ward were taken, and about a dozen native people stood or squatted outside, waiting their turn to see the doctor. The Jarai are animists who have their own traditional methods of healing; clearly, however, Dr. Smith had won their trust, and tribespeople walked long distances from their settlements to receive medical attention from her. It was evident, too, that she was very busy and focused on her work. Even so, she agreed to give me a few minutes of her time and listened attentively as I explained what I was doing and asked if she could help. She did, briefly, but explained that all her time was consumed by treating patients and running the hospital. Also, she did not want to jeopardize her work by being linked to the U.S. Army—good thinking on her part. I took my leave. On the drive back, I realized I had just had the distinct privilege of meeting an amazing woman, the Albert Schweitzer of Vietnam.

I learned recently that Dr. Smith stayed in Kontum another dozen years and left, in 1975, only when Kontum and South Vietnam were about to be overrun by the North Vietnamese Army. Before leaving, she adopted two young Montagnard children. Unlike Dr. Schweitzer, Pat Smith kept a low public profile and still remains little known to the American public. She died in 2005.

Cheo Reo

Another trip—this one in late February with a colleague—took me to Cheo Reo, a small logging village south of Pleiku outside of which a Special Forces camp had been established. Ed Ketterlinus and I—he had joined our field office and was to be my replacement—went there by helicopter, contour-flying at high speed very low over forests, fields, and Montagnard villages, whose inhabitants rushed out of their huts in amazement as we suddenly appeared and skimmed deafeningly over their heads. It was at Cheo Reo I learned the Central Intelligence Agency, rather than the army, was managing the operations of the Special Forces. Apparently, the Agency had the capability to establish these training camps more quickly and efficiently than the army, which was more burdened by bureaucracy and regulations. The Cheo Reo quartermaster sergeant, noting I was carrying only a sidearm, told me I should do better and offered me my pick of submachine guns, of which he had a considerable supply, including Swedish Ks and German Mausers. To my surprise, since they were supplied through the CIA, there was no accountability system for these weapons. I chose a Mauser, and plenty of ammunition.

After I returned stateside to my next assignment, I received a letter from a Central Registry compatriot in which he wrote that Ambassador Nolting had been replaced by Henry Cabot Lodge. Lodge, apparently, had qualms about the CIA's independence and undue influence in Vietnam, with the Special Forces having become almost its own militia, and he was in the process of rectifying the situation. As a result, as CIA operations were being dialed back, Central Registry was assuming some of its responsibilities.

That evening, while taking a stroll around the perimeter of the camp, Ed and I caught the strains of very unfamiliar music; it came from a small group of Montagnard auxiliaries, who were squatting around a campfire singing songs and playing handmade stringed instruments, including what resembled a single-stringed violin. The string, in fact, was a wire that ran along about a two-foot section of bamboo. One end of a short string was tied to the wire. A small shell disk was tied to the other end of the string. The player held the disk in his mouth. By pulling and releasing tension on the string, he was able to tighten and loosen tension on the wire and change the tone. He rubbed the wire with a wooden bow. The result was music such as I had never heard or imagined.

That night, sleeping on a cot in a large open-sided tent, I could hear rats scuttling around. The rat population in Vietnam in 1962–1963 was booming, and we all received bubonic plague inoculations.

Excerpt from a letter to my parents dated March 1, 1963:

Well, I'll be back next month ... makes it seem close; yesterday I got my orders to White Plains, N.Y., so it's pretty final. More boxes of clothing have arrived for the Montagnards ... lots of baby clothes which are perfect. Most of the clothing I have given to the missionaries since they have better access to the more needy people. I have a terrific photograph of a tribesman wearing a baseball jersey with YALE written across the chest ... a classic. One of the missionaries took it and is making me a couple of prints. [This was my father's jersey, which he had last worn in the 1927 Yale-Harvard baseball game.]

I just got back from a two day trip to Cheo Reo, a village in the province just south of Pleiku (new province so not on maps). It was a good trip. I was with another agent and we spent one day and night at the Special Forces training camp outside the village. We saw the Djarai tribesmen going through exercises and formations. After a short training, they are issued weapons and return to their native village as a home guard against the VC. It has worked very well in that area. During the evening Ed and I wandered through the native village next to the camp. This was very memorable. We walked up to one large group in the darkness and listened to them singing their tribal songs around the campfire. The houses, as you know from my pictures, are built up on stilts to keep them dry during the rainy season, and inside the people sit around small flickering fires at night and talk, or strum on native guitars or just sit. I imagine they are telling tales of days of old. I'd give anything to be able to speak freely (fluently) with the Montagnards. Later on, we walked down to the far end of the village and sat alone around a fire that someone had built. Half a dozen mongrel dogs came up and curled up next to us.

If I were to join the Army again I might well join the Special Forces [SF]. They are really an outfit to be very proud of, and I have been extremely impressed by the two outfits I

A Jarai man in a remote village, wearing my father's Yale baseball jersey.

Montagnard boys play around a bunker in a Jarai village.

116

have seen over here. They are the best soldiers in our military and among the best anywhere in the world. Also, by their very mission, they live in small groups (12) amongst tribespeople who need training and help. They do a lot of medical and social work ... every day natives come from all over to be cured of diseases and wounds. The requirements to enter and get through the SF training are so heavy that the quality of the men is very high. And they have terrific morale which comes from their being the best and doing an important challenging job and from working together closely in weird countries as a team for months and years. If I were going to become a professional soldier, I wouldn't be in any other outfit.

I saw an elephant in Cheo Reo. I was just looking out the window in the middle of town and there he was. He had a native sitting on his head riding him while he dragged a big log. I understand there are even some wild elephants around. A Frenchman I talked to slept out overnight when he was hunting in the forest and when he awoke there were wild elephants all around him!

This morning I got some good movies of some of our troops renewing their parachute jump training ... got right underneath them as they came down. It was the first time this has been done in Pleiku, and as you can imagine the poor Montagnards stood mouth-agape when they saw the spectacle. After this I went into town, where there was a big celebration going on...

There are two sisters who are very famous in Vietnamese history. They are the

Montagnard girls in Pleiku's Independence Day parade.

117

Part II

Joan of Arcs of Vietnam and rallied the army into combat to drive out the Chinese hoards several centuries ago. [Note: These were the Trung sisters, who lived in the first century CE] *So this holiday is in honor of them and all Vietnamese women. Here in Pleiku they make an effort to include the Montagnards in the program and bring them in by the truckloads from neighboring villages.*

They stand in rank for hours while the ceremony is going on. I asked one Djarai on the sidelines what it was all about and he didn't know. I spent the remainder of the morning with the missionaries talking photography and looking at their slides ... they really have some beauties as all three are avid photographers with the best equipment. By the way, I have just ordered a new camera and telephoto lens. It's a much better one than my old one which is about to fall apart. The whole outfit I'm getting costs over $200.00 in Hong Kong and about double that retail at home, so you can imagine the quality of it all. The camera's a Canon (Japanese). It'll be a lifetime investment. You know too that I bought a movie camera ... it is working out very well and I've already taken about 200 feet of film all in color. It's a Bell & Howell with a 1.8 Zoom (telescopic) lens and electric eye light meter (automatic) and cost only $59.00 at the PX ... this is also about half retail price. So I've done OK for camera equipment. I plan to learn how to develop and print as soon as I can.

Per usual there is no news to tell of the war over here. It just drags on and on with no noticeable changes to speak of. You don't know who they are or where they are or where they'll attack next, and in my opinion the reason is because our (Vietnamese) intelligence is lousy. I think this is a key to our success, and until we get a positive

Amidst a flurry of confetti, young Vietnamese women place leis around the necks of Vietnamese soldiers on Independence Day in Pleiku.

118

intelligence operation which can answer those three questions, we will continue to suffer embarrassing minor defeats. And this is a field which has to be done by the Vietnamese. The first thing I was told when I came over here was watch out for the VC. I asked how I could recognize one and the reply was, "Oh, that's easy ... they look just like the Vietnamese." Well, this problem can work in just the reverse manner, but the entire operation over here is oriented in too much of a defensive way. You do not have to penetrate North Vietnam to penetrate VC territory, and the loyal Vietnamese look just like VC. The Vietnamese are cautious and hesitant people (unlike Americans), and as many frustrated American officers and NCOs who work and fight with them will tell you, they are afraid to close with the enemy. Well, enough politics.

Ban Me Thuot and Phan Thiet

The town of Ban Me Thuot (also spelled Buon Ma Thuot), south of Pleiku, known as the Montagnard capital, was in the heart of Rhadé country. I needed to conduct some security-clearance interviews at the U.S. Army post there. Because the country between Pleiku and Ban Me Thuot was largely under Viet Cong control, travel overland was too dangerous, so I had to fly. As it happened, Major General Ton That Dinh was scheduled to fly there, and he gave permission for me to travel with him. I reported to the airport well before departure and found that besides the general and several aides and bodyguards, I would be the only passenger. On board, an aide introduced me to the general, after which we had no more contact, his seat being forward and mine in the rear. He was in his thirties and, like the Pleiku police chief, of small stature. Even his hat seemed oversized for his body. His uniform was covered with ribbons. In the air, tea was served and offered to me, as well.

As we doglegged to land at the Ban Me Thuot airfield, I saw that it was no more than a landing strip cut into the forest. There was no town in sight. We deplaned and I held back while the general strutted across the tarmac waving his swagger stick, his retinue clustered around. Then I followed at an appropriate distance. I entered the small terminal building, where a swarm of district military officers and petty provincial officials were waiting to greet the general.

Eventually, the knot of people moved out to the front of the building, where a military motorcade had formed—a black sedan, troop trucks, security vehicles of various types, and jeeps. When all was ready, the general climbed into his car, soldiers waved their arms, whistles blew, and doors slammed.

Part II

As I watched the activity from the front entrance, impressed by the ritual, someone on the general's staff asked me if I needed transportation into Ban Me Thuot. He said the town was ten miles away and I realized that soon I would be standing by myself in an empty airport in the boondocks. I accepted his offer of a ride. The officer motioned for me to wait while he went to speak with the general. Moments later, an order was barked out. The aide came back and informed me that a jeep and driver had been arranged for me at the tail end of the motorcade. We soon moved out.

We drove through the countryside for several kilometers, then entered woods where presently I began to notice Montagnards gathered along the side of the road. As we approached Ban Me Thuot, their numbers increased—men, women, and children, all standing and waving and applauding as we passed. Of course, this was a planned, orchestrated event; nevertheless, it had a celebratory atmosphere and was even continuing when my own jeep passed by.

At first, I slouched down in embarrassment and tried to look inconspicuous. But these Rhadé Montagnards, who had had the courtesy (more likely had been ordered) to leave their villages to greet us, knew nothing of my true status. And who knows how long they had been patiently squatting along the road. So, I decided: Hey, lighten up, Noble—enjoy your brief moment of fame! And so, with dignified restraint, I saluted the crowds. Then, loosening up more, I smiled, waved, and clasped my hands together to show solidarity. Finally, as we entered Ban Me Thuot itself and the crowds swelled deep along the streets, I threw out Ike's V-for-victory sign. And so it was that Private First Class Noble, now posing as a celebrity arrived into the provincial capital of Ban Me Thuot.

My driver dropped me off at the MAAG compound, which I found to be not the ordinary sterile army-issue complex of barracks and huts; rather, it was built up off the ground of timbers and boards and was clearly inspired by the style of Rhadé houses, only much scaled up. It was a truly impressive structure, designed with cultural sensitivity and imagination.

I presented myself to the commander and requested lodging and told him why I was there—to conduct a couple of routine security-clearance interviews. He made it clear that he had little use for the CIC, but I was welcome to stay. His sergeant showed me to a comfortable room opening onto the second-story balcony.

The following day, after the interviews, I caught a flight on an Otter—one of the Canadian bush planes the army was using in Vietnam—to another army post, in Phan Thiet, to conduct more security interviews.

On the way, when we encountered a towering thunderstorm, the pilot circled numerous times until the small plane rose over the top of the clouds and went on. Before landing bumpily in a field, he made several low passes to chase off grazing buffalo. In Phan Thiet, I was to investigate a security problem: Viet Cong snipers shooting at aircraft from the end of the runway.

At the Phan Thiet post, I shared lodging in a small cottage with Malcolm Browne, the Associated Press's chief correspondent in Indochina, who was investigating the same incidents. (Browne was later awarded a Pulitzer Prize for his reporting in Vietnam.) The next day, after briefing us on the security problem, the commanding officer gave us a tour of Phan Thiet and surrounding area, a highlight of which was a ruin from the ancient Champa kingdom perched on a cliff overlooking the sea. Seeing this impressive tower made me realize more than ever how little I knew about Vietnam's deep history and rich civilization. We also passed downwind of a malodorous factory that made *nuoc mam*, the ubiquitous fermented fish sauce.

Through the day, Malcolm Browne and I got on friendly informal terms. As an experienced reporter who had been in Saigon for a couple of years, he was very well informed about what was going on in Vietnam and Southeast Asia. After dinner, we moved to the officers' lounge to join a group of Australian rangers who were stationed in Phan Thiet. While we downed a few pints of lager, they regaled us with stories until late in the evening. Later still, in our bunks, Malcolm and I talked for a long time during which he shared a wealth of experiences and information with me. I learned, for example, that the Viet Cong had a thriving trade in opium, transported from the Golden Triangle (an opium-growing region that includes areas of Thailand, Burma, and Laos), and this enterprise was helping to finance their operations in Vietnam: opium was their currency. Talking with him, I felt like a complete novice, which, indeed, I was.

A Week in Saigon

From Phan Thiet, I went on to Saigon, where, in contrast to my arrival months before, I was welcomed at Central Registry. Gallagher himself emerged from his office with a warm greeting. When the agents I had come over with expressed eagerness to hear what it was like up country, I realized how trapped they were feeling by the dull routine at headquarters. Also, the outfit was continuing to grow. One newcomer at the office, who had inherited my old copying job, said he had a bone to pick with me. It seemed he'd been assigned the job of copying a long informative *New Yorker* article my mother had sent me earlier, "A Reporter in Vietnam: The Delta, the Plateau, and the Mountains," by Robert Shaplen. After reading it, I had passed it along to a colleague in the office, who had given it to someone else, and so on until it had landed on Gallagher's desk. Apparently, it had impressed him enough that he had ordered it copied in multiples. Mother was surprised and proud to learn that her clipping had become required reading by every incoming counterintelligence agent in South Vietnam.

Excerpts from a letter to my father dated November 6, 1962:

> *You might be pleased to hear that I sent that long newspaper article about Vietnam* [Note: This was a different article from the *New Yorker* piece], *which you had typed up, down to my headquarters as background information for new agents arriving in the country. They must have been impressed by it as they stenciled the whole article and have distributed it around through intelligence channels. A real contribution on your part to our effort over here. Many thanks.*
>
> *P.S. My boss in Saigon made a remark in the presence of other agents which I pass on to you. He said, "I'd go anywhere with Kuhn and Noble. Those two know their business."*

Of course, Gallagher's comment pleased me as I had never heard him utter a compliment about anyone; however, the fact is, he never went anywhere with Rob and me and had he come to Pleiku and witnessed Kuhn's deteriorated condition (see pages 127–129), his assessment might have been otherwise.

I checked into the Continental Palace to find "my" former suite now cluttered with cots being used by new agents—another sign that things were changing. The buildup was under way. None of the newcomers spoke Vietnamese or French nor, it appeared to me, did they have the kind of background and experience that would enable them to operate effectively in Vietnam. A couple, however, were Nisei—at least they could blend physically into the population better than the rest of us.

I looked forward to seeing Kumar, who recently had been promoted to lieutenant colonel, and, as luck would have it, he was in Saigon. We met to have dinner and took a cab to Cholon, where he had discovered a Japanese restaurant he liked. There I had my first taste of sake. After dinner, as before, we went on a walkabout and renewed our friendship. This was the last time I saw him, for he was due soon to return to India. Regrettably, we lost contact and never heard from each other again.

The following morning, I met Malcolm Browne for breakfast in a small café near the hotel. While we were chatting, David Halberstam of the *New York Times* joined us. Afterward, Malcolm brought me to his cramped office, where I met Peter Arnett. Other than Browne, with whom I had just spent time, I'd never heard of these young reporters, who later won Pulitzer prizes and became famous (although loathed by some) for their coverage of the war.

Later in the morning, at Central Registry, I wrote up my agent reports from Ban Me Thuot and Phan Thiet. Gallagher received them and, upon reading about the Viet Cong financing their war by trading in opium, he summoned me and demanded to know how I had learned this information. When I revealed that my source was Malcolm Browne, his face darkened and grew darker still when I mentioned we had shared a room for two nights. I didn't mention the drinking and late-night discussion. The press, it became abundantly clear, was anathema to Gallagher; he told me that whatever I had said to Browne would soon appear on the AP wire services credited to "an official government source." He glared at me and shook his head in dismay. "That's you." (I also did not mention having had breakfast with Browne and Halberstam that morning.) Gallagher instructed me to have no further contact whatsoever with Browne or any other correspondent. When he saw the astonishment in my expression, he added, "That's a direct order. If you see him walking down the sidewalk, cross the street." He then called a staff meeting and repeated the directive to everyone.

Part II

In having spoken to a member of the press, I had apparently crossed a line into the territory of a different enemy. What the commander said struck fear in me for, as I thought back on Browne's and my frank conversation, I realized I may have said some things that could be quoted in a news story. A week or two passed before my anxiety over this began to fade and I knew I was in the clear.

Browne and Halberstam were doing pretty much what I was doing—foraging for information about the situation in South Vietnam. The difference, of course, was that they were better at it than I was. For one thing, they were living on the economy and knew their way around and were better able to develop local sources of information. Their articles were controversial, but, in my view, they reported on the war responsibly and should be credited for offering the American public more objective perspectives on what was happening than were being provided by the Department of Defense. They were often criticized by hawkish politicians and columnists; Neil Sheehan, the *Newsweek* correspondent, in fact, was thrown out of the country by the Diem regime, which objected to his reporting aspects of the war that were going badly. Still today, I feel privileged in having briefly crossed paths with these foreign correspondents.

As the military buildup in Vietnam continued, flights upcountry became more difficult to arrange, and I found myself stuck for nearly a week in Saigon with little to do. When I did finally get on a flight, bad weather conditions in Pleiku forced the pilot to turn around and go back to Saigon. Back in September, how eager I had been to leave the city and get away from drudge work at headquarters, but now, with spare time on my hands, Saigon seduced me, and Pleiku seemed bleak by contrast.

The more time I spent in Vietnam, the more I wished I spoke Vietnamese and the Montagnard languages and knew more about the country's history and culture. In this regard, my missionary friends were helpful, and also Captain Bang. In Pleiku, Bang had taken me to an opera performed by a small itinerant company. The venue, a kind of community grange hall, was packed with enthusiastic town and country folk. I was the only foreigner. The tale revolved around a warrior and a damsel in distress and was replete with romance and melodrama. The illusionary effects included a flame-spouting dragon and a broad glittering rug that rotated vertically on rollers to form a credible waterfall. The audience was beside itself with enthusiasm.

Noticing my delight in this modest rural presentation, Bang wanted me to experience the *real thing*, in Saigon. As it happened, he was in the capital on leave while I was still waiting for a flight back to Pleiku, and he and his wife treated me to a performance at the National Opera.

It was a large beautiful opera house, and the crowd included many of Saigon's elite. As for the performance, it was a far cry from what I had witnessed in Pleiku; this was classical Vietnamese opera—highly stylized, interminably long, and, to me, incomprehensible. Not even Bang's whispered explanations of what was happening helped much. I found it to be a very tedious affair, indeed.

Excerpt from a letter to my family dated December 18, 1962:

Merry Christmas! Or Happy New Year, if this arrives late. I'll be thinking of you all together.

I'm in Saigon, letting off some steam after two months straight in the boonies. As a matter of fact, I let off so much last night that I was all steamed out this morning when I had an appointment to call you. But I've rationalized since [then] to the effect you would have been out or too surprised to say anything if at home.

… I found that after 2 months with the tribesmen of the High Plateau I am utterly floored by the Saigon women. There is no doubt they are the most beautiful & alluring females in the world. In fact, it is quite upsetting, after being isolated, to be confronted by such excitement as they inspire and I will be most relieved to see the dust and dirty feet of the Montagnards again.

… Our new boss arrived yesterday and will assume command in 2 weeks. Gallagher will be famous for the job he has done here. He will return to Holabird to join the faculty and be promoted. Of course, it is the sort of fame one never reads about—the man behind the scenes sort of thing.

A new man I met in headquarters, Peter Spalding, persuaded me to go to church with him on Sunday; in fact, the Episcopal/Anglican church was only a few blocks from the Continental Palace, but despite its being a good place to meet people, maybe even an American girl, I had never been to it. Spalding came from a diplomatic family, so he was "in" with the embassy crowd. After the service, he introduced me to Ambassador and Mrs. Nolting, who invited me to a Christmas party at their house on December 23. That would have offered quite a different view of Vietnam! By then, however, I would be back in Pleiku. Besides, Gallagher probably would have forbidden "fraternization" with an ambassador.

A colleague at headquarters told me that Major Gallagher considered me his most effective agent working in the field. My head swelled and I made some comment about being the lowest ranking guy in the outfit. He replied that I should put in for a field commission and that if I completed the paperwork before Gallagher left, I would probably soon find myself a second lieutenant. So, I picked up the forms.

Life in Pleiku

Sometimes, USO (United Service Organization) performers showed up at the Pleiku MAAG to entertain us. On one occasion, it was America's ping pong champion; he toured military bases with an appealing young female assistant whose role was to wear a skimpy outfit and retrieve stray balls. The champ would challenge anyone in the audience to a game, which, of course, he would easily win. The assistant, according to rumor among the troops, had an after-performance assignation with the ranking officer at each camp. When I mentioned the upcoming show to Captain Bang, he expressed a desire to attend. Why? I asked. "Because I'm Vietnam's ping pong champion," he coolly replied. I knew that Asians were the best players in the world, so I set it up: As I visualized it, Bang would come and sit in the audience, accept the American's challenge, and crush him.

I couldn't wait for the show, and when I told Rob what was in the offing, we discussed taking side bets in the officers' lounge. Unfortunately, two problems arose: I was sent on an assignment to Nha Trang, and Bang was called out of town, too. The USO champ never knew how close he came to being humiliated.

Another USO show, billing itself as "The Fastest Painter Alive," featured an artist who created paintings in record time. He performed in the NCO lounge, where I had a front-row seat. The fellow had a well-honed stage presence and pizzazz and joked with the soldiers as he painted one memorized scene after another with lightning speed. His pièce de résistance, I remember, executed blindfolded on a large Masonite board, depicted a lake surrounded by trees and snow-capped mountains in the distance. He even included a deer drinking from the still waters. Years later, my wife and I were listening to National Public Radio and heard an interview with this same performer; he was still at it, playing hotels in the Catskills. "Hey," I told her, "Listen to this—it's the same guy who came to Pleiku!"

The USO sent us a musical show, too, with a sizeable cast of actors.

I invited Captain and Mrs. Bang to attend with me. To my dismay and embarrassment, it turned out to be a bawdy, vulgar, sexist revue featuring striptease dancers and rotten humor aimed to amuse horny GIs. I was thankful that neither of them understood English. Afterward, as we passed the officers' lounge, I said, "Would you like to come in for a drink?" "Yes," Bang replied. So, I stepped in and held the door open. But, to my surprise, they walked on. This was another lesson: in Asia, it's impolite to answer a question in the negative—yes can mean no.

At my request, my mother sent me a bundle of back issues of the Sunday *New York Times Magazine*. I was very out of touch with world news and I did, indeed, want to read the magazine's articles. An underlying motive, however, was to ogle the models in the ads. In truth, I was a lonely oversexed young male stuck in the boondocks with an older ornery partner; so, to glimpse a few pictures of fashion models was something to look forward to. Doesn't that seem innocent now with the proliferation of sexually explicit ads in the media and pornography on the Internet! Well, Mother came through partway: a stack of magazines soon arrived. However, to reduce postage costs, she had snipped out all the ads.

There were two occasions in Pleiku when we were all placed on high alert. One was when word spread that a major attack was imminent. Supposedly, the Chinese had entered the war. Rob and I stayed in our room and shut the door and got out the Mauser and clips. Nothing happened: a false rumor. The second time was when President Kennedy spoke to the nation during the Cuban Missile Crisis. One of the officers brought his shortwave radio to the bar and fiddled with the dials until we could hear the faint but familiar sound of Kennedy's voice. It was an electrifying moment; his voice came in strong, then faded or disappeared in static, then surged back. I remember the tension in the room more than the content of his speech. Someone remarked that we were safer in Vietnam than we would be in America.

Rob Kuhn liked to drink. And he did—a lot. Around five o'clock we would shut the office door and walk down the hill to the officers' lounge with our booklets of drink chits. At ten cents for a beer and a quarter for a shot of hard liquor, drinking cost hardly more than breathing. At the commissary, alcohol could be purchased even cheaper by the bottle than at the bar. The officers' lounge became Rob's regular hangout. He had his favorite spot at a corner of the bar, where he would sit for hours drinking Chivas Regal and chatting with the bartender or whoever happened to be nearby.

For that matter, drinking was the main off-duty pastime for quite a few of the officers in the MAAG compound. After work, it was cocktail hour, and then we would move on to the mess for dinner. Occasionally, there would be a steak cookout in the garden of the quadrangle, which, apparently, had been designed by Colonel Wilson himself. The officers' mess had tables for four, as well as a larger head table where the colonel held court in the company of his higher-ranking officers. Clueless about senior-officer protocols and politics, I stayed away from the head table and only sat there when no other seating was available. Even then I did not speak unless spoken to, which rarely happened, for conversation revolved around the commander.

After dinner, it was usually back to the bar for Rob. I generally returned to our room and read a book or wrote letters. As I commented in a January 10 letter to my parents, "Well, the holiday season is over. I'm glad of it, too. The emphasis in a place like this is on boozing, and not being much of a boozer myself, I found it quite a strain." An alternate evening pastime was to watch a movie in the NCO lounge. The offerings were hardly new releases: Audie Murphy playing himself in a World War II adventure, Gary Cooper as Sergeant York, or a well-worn western. Most of the MAAG personnel were officers—captains and majors—who were serving as advisors to their Vietnamese counterparts in II Corps. There were fewer enlisted men, all of whom, as I recall, were non-commissioned officers. Regardless of rank, we all had plenty of time to kill after work and in the evenings, and for many at MAAG it was filled by drinking, movies, or both.

As time went on, Rob Kuhn drank more heavily, both at the bar and from a bottle in our quarters. Often, he would drink himself to oblivion and pass out on his bunk, fully dressed. In the mornings, severely hung over and in a sour humor, he'd manage to pull himself together. As this continued, he grew ill-humored and, increasingly, cross with me, especially when he stumbled back to the room and found me writing a letter or reading a literary type of book. He began criticizing me in personal ways ("What the fuck are you reading *now*!") and pulled rank to humiliate me. For example, he would find a typo in a draft report I had written and order me to retype the whole thing. Since I was doing all the fieldwork, I was producing all the reports. His job was to read them and send them on to headquarters in Saigon.

This situation, although workable professionally, undermined our personal relationship, and I had no recourse. I didn't know what to do, for there were just the two of us and I was the underling. To manage the situation, I kept out of his way as much as I could. Sometimes, I would go to the Blue Spring Bar in Pleiku, but often, anticipating his return from the officers' lounge, I would lie on my bunk and pretend to be asleep. He knew I was avoiding him and accused me of being conceited. If disliking a person and trying to hold on to a bit of privacy and self-respect was being stuck-up, then yes, I was guilty as charged.

Eventually, the alcohol intake made Rob physically ill. For hours, sometimes for days, he would lie on his cot and sleep, sitting up only to have the dry heaves, leaning over a wastebasket sweating and retching. Unable to hold down food, he would cease eating altogether. He looked ill, his complexion became gray, he grew weak and unsteady on his feet, his hands trembled, and his moods were erratic. When he had his first spell of vomiting, I didn't realize it was from alcohol poisoning and urged him to see a doctor. He refused, no doubt fearing the doctor would recognize the symptoms of alcoholism and possibly report him. During the days he was bedridden, I covered for him, staying in the office to answer the phone and making reasons for his absence in the lounge and the mess hall. For me, by far the toughest aspect of my life in Pleiku was sharing a single room and workspace with this older, depressed, hostile, alcoholic master sergeant. My philosophy was to muddle through and count the days to the end of my tour.

Excerpt from a letter to George H. Hobson in Paris, dated February 18, 1963.

HOWDY yourself!! Glad to hear you so caught up in your writing and inspired with your creativity. For this alone your year abroad is an invaluable success. I have over here found good writing material ... characters, situations, plots, moods ... and have been at times eager to try it out. But myself, I have not the proper atmosphere. As I breathlessly launch into expressing an idea, my Brooklyn-cop boss will come crashing into the only room of ours with too many beers under his belt and [in a] nasty mood equally eager to boil out in a stream of blasphemy. He does not like me and he probably knows the sentiment is mutual. He is suspicious of my occasionally writing long letters ... suspicious of the fact that I have thoughts and feelings and perceptions which have not occurred to him because he doesn't have a Yale education. So I have for a long time now not even tempted myself with writable thoughts ... except now and again. My fear is that when I leave this dust bowl/swamp it will take a great deal to relive it enough in my imagination to recreate it in words. We shall see.

Plei Mrong
Is Dedicated

Plei Mrong was a Montagnard village that had been modified into a "strategic hamlet," which included a Special Forces camp led by Captain William Grace. Also participating were Vietnamese Civilian Irregular Defense Group fighters and a Bahnar Strike Force. Their mission was to train young Jarai men to defend themselves and their villages from the Viet Cong. Shortly before Christmas, Rob and I were invited to attend its dedication. True to form, he elected not to go.

In 1962, the strategic hamlet program was South Vietnam's new approach to defeating the Viet Cong and winning the war. It was modeled on a counterinsurgency concept that had been employed by the British in Malaya. President Diem's brother, Ngo Dinh Nhu, ran it, in collaboration with our Central Intelligence Agency. The idea was to transform farming villages into defensive compounds with perimeter fences and moats filled with *bungi* stakes, which were sharpened bamboo spikes. In many cases, the government uprooted Montagnards from their home villages and resettled them elsewhere, where they were supplied with rifles and trained to use them. A dark-hour curfew was imposed, as well. If successful, the VC would be unable any longer to appropriate food and other supplies and propagandize and recruit the villagers. Due to their location in the Central Highlands and close to the so-called Ho Chi Minh Highway, a network of supply trails leading south from North Vietnam along the remote borders of Laos and Cambodia, Pleiku and Kontum provinces were key to the strategy's success. It was a sound concept but hard to put into practice. Although it achieved some initial successes, this approach to defeating an insurgency ultimately failed.

I drove out to Plei Mrong on a Saturday morning just before Christmas with Captain Richard Edwards, an American Intelligence officer. We arrived about the same time as a host of military and civil officials, embassy and CIA representatives, foreign correspondents, and hundreds of Jarai and Bahnar tribespeople, who were streaming in from villages in the surrounding countryside. It was clear that this strategic-hamlet dedication had been planned as a major public relations affair and Camp Plei Mrong was to be a regional showpiece in the program. Two water buffaloes had been readied for the throngs of Montagnards who arrived from surrounding villages, and an elaborate meal was prepared for the Vietnamese and American guests.

Before speeches by dignitaries started, I walked around the village to see how it looked and do some photography, using my mother's old Zeiss Ikon and my newly acquired Bell and Howell movie camera. No one expressed an objection to being photographed although four elders, whom I asked to take their portrait, showed no interest in what I was doing.

I had been in the Highlands for more than three months and already my attitude toward the Montagnards had evolved; whereas I first viewed them as backward, primitive, and impoverished, now I saw them—my photographs reflect this—as handsome dignified people with their own distinct cultural traditions and strong family ties. The men were generally of short stature, trim and muscular. They wore loincloths and shirts of

Indigenous tribespeople gather in Plei Mrong, bringing bungi stakes for village defense.

131

Four village elders in the village of Plei Mrong.

hand-woven black striped fabric, and they smoked long-stemmed pipes. Their houses were beautifully designed from local materials—timbers, sticks, and grass—and were built on poles. I was particularly struck by a tall elegant house with a steeply pitched roof that was the residence, I was told, of unmarried men. The family houses often had a porch, or balcony, where women would weave cloth on a loom. Beneath the floors, firewood could be stacked and cows, pigs, and goats could take shelter. I also passed some barracks where the Jarai trainees lived, and entered one where I was able, even in the dim light, to photograph some young soldiers hanging out and cleaning their rifles.

A ceremony, including the ritual slaughter of a water buffalo, was held in the village center. After that, the Vietnamese and Americans guests banqueted under an awning, while some of the Jarai men feasted separately a short distance off. They dragged the sacrificed buffalo away, hacking chunks of meat off the carcass, and roasted it over an open fire on their

Opposite top: A special house in Plei Mrong where unmarried young men lived. *Opposite bottom:* Bahnar Strike Force soldiers in their barracks in Plei Mrong's Special Forces camp.

132

Jarai Montagnards with ceramic jars of rice wine, a favorite beverage of the indigenous people, especially following the harvest.

bayonets. The Montagnards also had brought with them an abundance of tall ceramic amphorae filled with rice wine. The jars were over two feet in height with a neck about three inches high.

Missionaries, including Charlie Long and Victor Oliver, condemned the natives' custom of consuming large amounts of rice wine as both immoral and wasteful (of rice and time) and preached against it. However, getting drunk after the harvest was a deeply entrenched cultural tradition. Following their buffalo feast, the Jarai headmen invited some of us to join them in drinking from their huge jugs of rice wine. I felt it would be rude to refuse, and besides, I was curious. I sat in a chair by an amphora alongside the main chief, or shaman, and sucked the brew up through a long bamboo straw that went all the way down to the murky bottom of the jar. I confess to some apprehension about doing this, not so much for the foul taste and questionable ingredients than for fear of being exposed to TB or leprosy from the bamboo tube, which had already been used by previous imbibers. Fortunately, a few swigs of Scotch from a friend's flask, boosted my courage.

The chief was a sullen looking individual who resembled a surly Anthony Quinn. He watched me closely as I drank, and made monosyllabic utterances indicating he would tolerate no efforts to fake sucking in the fluid; this was a serious ritual. After managing the first few gulps, a problem arose—the quantity I was expected to drink was too much for the capacity of my stomach, which was already full from eating, and the mixture began to rise up in my throat. Pride can motivate remarkable feats, but, in this case, my swallowing reflex simply shut down. Puffing my cheeks in and out to simulate swallowing did not fool the shaman, who made more negative guttural sounds. He was a strong figure of a man armed with a long machete that hung in a scabbard from his belt, which he had used an hour earlier to kill a water buffalo. When I felt close to vomiting, I closed my eyes and forced more of the distasteful concoction down my throat. Satisfied at last, the chief grinned broadly, encircled my wrist with a brass bracelet, and gave a concluding benefaction as he poured buffalo blood on my shoe. I had passed the test and, as someone told me, been initiated into the tribe. I was also told to keep the bracelet on for it would bring lasting good health. I took all this seriously and the bracelet remained on my wrist for many years. Occasionally, at unexpected times, back in America, a Vietnam vet who had served with the Montagnards would notice it and, knowing its significance, ask where in the Highlands I had been stationed. I was particularly counting on its powers when I underwent major surgery in 1990; however, despite my objections, a nurse in the operating room removed it. (The surgery went well anyway.) By 1994, it had worn too thin to keep on, and I now store it in a box.

A letter to my family, Christmas Eve, 1962:

Dear Family,

Your cards arrived this afternoon and were just given to me. What perfect timing! Tomorrow I'll open the presents. This is such a different Christmas for me that I really can hardly believe that it is Christmas. I want to write you about two Christmas parties that I went to, as they, and especially one, will forever be one of the great experiences of my life and certainly an experience known to very few Americans.

I was invited to attend the dedication ceremonies of the Plei Mrong Training Camp which is run by our Special Forces about 30 kms. to the north-east of Pleiku in country which is full of VC. I went out with a good friend named Captain Edwards who is the U.S. Intelligence Advisor for the province. We arrived at the village about 9:30 and I spent about an hour wandering about the village taking pictures of the houses and people. It is a Djarai village. At 11:00 the ceremonies began. Eight Djarai villages had been invited as well as some big wheels from the U.S. embassy and the Province Chief and some Vietnamese VIPs. From all around the area Djarai came in walking single file and carrying on their backs food and rice wine. There were hundreds and hundreds of them congregated in Plei Mrong. Until noon there were some briefings and speeches and such after which we were escorted to a training area about a mile away. We passed through 1000 meters of fields where as far as you could see the Viet Cong had placed a sea of bamboo spears into the ground and set ground traps to impale Government forces. We had to pick our way along very slowly so as not to get spiked. We got back to the village about 1:00 p.m. and the fun was just beginning ...

The Djarai had brought in two buffaloes to be sacrificed as an offering to their spirits. They had been there all morning tied to sacrificial poles just at the edge of the village. Next to them were rows of jugs of rice wine. When I got back the Djarai had begun a tribal dance in preparation for the sacrifice. They beat on brass gongs of all sizes and tones ... a weird, primitive throbbing music with a fabulous beat

These bungi stakes (sharpened bamboo sticks) were placed in a field near the hamlet of Plei Mrong by the Viet Cong to impede troop movements.

which sends you into reveries of the exotic and primeval. The men danced along in a line around the buffaloes while the young children stood around the ring in which the sacrifice was about to take place. Two Djarai chiefs, dressed in loin cloths and carrying elaborate shields and long knives, were sparring in the middle of the ring, acting out a mock battle. All this was done in a crouching, jumping, stalking dance step in rhythm with the throb of the brass gongs. Suddenly, upon a signal from someone in the crowd, the two chiefs closed in on one of the buffaloes and slashed open the tendons in the back of the hind legs. They continued their dance while the tribespeople cheered and roared with laughter. They closed in again, slashing here and there but particularly around the legs and shoulders. With their tendons severed and the muscles in their legs opened up, the buffalo thrashed around frantically on its elbows and knees. Blood poured from wounds in the neck and shoulders, and it sagged down upon its side. The dance and cheers continued…. Finally the chiefs began giving the coup de grace to the buffalo by trying to stab their long machete-like knives deep into the heart. The animal died. Tribesmen gathered

around and tied a rope around its head and dragged it off. The same ritual was enacted with the second buffalo.

I might add a word about my activities during this thing. I had a movie camera, all of which's film I had just used up, and my Zeiss Ikon, which had three pictures left. I managed to get at the inner edge of the ring, about five or ten yards from the struggle. After taking my three pictures, I frantically began changing films, my heart pounding and hands trembling with excitement. I broke my camera in the process and of course missed pictures, which only lucky missionaries have had the opportunity to take, in ages past. I finally did get the second film in and took a few of the dead animals and I am awaiting the results now. It's possible that the whole film will be overexposed, as I broke off the back of my camera in my haste. C'est la vie.

A large banquet had been prepared for us. (The Djarai rushed off to eat the buffaloes which is the last part of the sacrificial

Montagnard dancers at the ceremony to dedicate the Special Forces training camp at Plei Mrong, located in a remote area between Pleiku and Kontum.

Part II

Two Montagnard chiefs killing a water buffalo as a ritual sacrifice. This was part of a ceremony during the dedication of a Special Forces training camp in Plei Mrong.

ceremony.) We had a bottle of whiskey, of Cognac, and of wine at the table and all kinds of beer. A Vietnamese District Chief sitting opposite me filled my water glass up with whiskey and ice, so before I knew it I was feeling no pain. Also, I needed the drink to help me work up an appetite. Soup, roast pig, roast duck and an assortment of other dishes were laid out before us, and before we knew it we were drunk and well satisfied. After lunch the dignitaries departed. Edwards and I and two other majors decided to stay and join the Djarai during their impending party. Also there was the team of Special Forces who are a terrific bunch of fellows as well as the best American soldiers in existence. Also there was a UPI reporter from Saigon named Neil Sheehan. I started taking photographs and before I knew it was being forcibly invited by the Djarai to partake of their rice wine which they had in many great jugs all around.

I must set aside a part here and try and describe Djarai rice wine. It is made with spring water and rice and is drunk in great quantity ... great quantity. The amount of it which a man can consume is relative to his power and strength as a man. So drinking rice wine with the Djarai is not only a challenge but also a contest and a very drunk one indeed. The jug is about two feet high and has a neck which is about seven inches in diameter. A piece of split bamboo is laid over the top and in the split is set a sliver of bamboo pointing down into the jug. This sliver is 1.5 inches long. The idea is to drink down the wine non-stop until the bottom of the bamboo sliver is entirely out of the wine. Thus, the sliver acts as a measuring stick, and if you do not understand the above explanation, the end result is that to drink to the bottom of the bamboo once is equal to consuming about one and one half water glasses of wine. I might add that the wine is more than wine. It is grass,

138

Guests enjoy a luncheon banquet at the Plei Mrong dedication event.

Montagnards feasting on one of the slaughtered buffaloes.

weeds, wood, rice and an assortment of other materials whose identity I am glad I do not know. One of these I was told by a Vietnamese is the raw blood of the animal. This I quite believe as I think I tasted a rich heavy substance in the wine along with the rest.

139

Part II

Ritual drinking of rice wine. From left to right: a Montagnard chieftain; a Vietnamese ranger; Captain William Grace, commander of the Plei Mrong Special Forces team.

By the time I had finished I had polished off six measures. The Djarai love to get Americans drunk. In fact, the Djarai equivalent to "Hello" is "Let's get drunk." Well, we did. On my second jug a chief came up to me, squatted at my feet while I drank, and poured fresh blood from the buffalo on my right foot, smeared it around, and mumbled a prayer to the spirits. I found out later that this is an honor, and the prayer is meant to protect you from evil spirits, including the VC, which are to me a bit more real than the spirits. On the fifth jug I saw a formidable looking Djarai who was identified to me as the chief of all the Djarai villages. So with my mind always on duty, I went over and introduced myself. I was greeted with an "ugh" and given his bamboo straw and a measuring stick. His wine was considerably stronger than the rest. I got down several slugs when all the slugs from the previous five jugs began ascending rapidly up into my throat. So I stopped in order to get my bearings, and the chief came out with a rather severe sounding monologue, which was translated to me in French by a Vietnamese who spoke Djarai to the effect that "The chief, he chew your ass because you stop drinking wine." So I slugged it all down and afterwards was presented with a tribal bracelet which is considered an honor to receive. I was very honored, especially since it was presented to me by the chief of the village and the chief of the whole Djarai tribe. I shall always keep it.

During the whole drinking period, which lasted for about two hours, the tribesmen dance around us in a circle beating on the gongs and drums. One Special

140

Forces sergeant was wildly intoxicated and joined the dance, adding to its regular pulse a strain of American "Twist" and "Rock and Roll." The Djarai thought this was terrific.... I wonder if it'll catch on. The Djarai are terribly friendly and really like Americans. Their mentality is closer to that of the Westerner than the Vietnamese. They are open and frank and honest and love a good time. Basically I much prefer them to the Vietnamese. Later, two of the villagers asked me out to look over the town and of course we ended up at the local pub ... a straw hut where we bought some Vietnamese beer.

Well, we finally headed back in time to reach the camp before darkness. The Special Forces there were worried about us and wanted us to stay the night and go back in the morning. The trip went without incident ... maybe thanks to the blessing of the Djarai medicine man. After we got back, the party went on and on and on at the MAAG bar and at the local hot spot in Pleiku. It was inspired by a pretty blond foreign correspondent from the New York Times who had just arrived from Laos. I only remember snatches here and there but made it to bed at some time because I woke up there the following morning and made it to church. Charlie Long, one of the local missionaries, brought his Djarai choir which he has taught to sing Christmas carols in Djarai in four parts. It was really fabulous to hear and very touching. They did very well, singing Silent Night and a few others. Needless to say the rest of Sunday was spent trying to recover. But as it turned out I had to pay some visits during the afternoon and do some entertaining with local types.

Today is Monday and several of us went out to a Djarai village nearby where they were having a fiesta ... lots of rice wine. I managed to get by with only enough wine to be polite ... it's foul tasting stuff. Took many photos and passed out some clothing which was most appreciated!! It's just too wonderful to see a tiny little poor tribal girl putting on a new red and white calico or gingham dress. It means a lot to them. Especially now, the weather is quite cool. And we had the village in the palm of our hand after that. I carried kids around on my shoulders and bounced them on my knee, drank wine with the men, and even danced with two of the girls. About 4:00 they brought out the gongs and started playing music and dancing. I was standing by watching and one woman came over and insisted that I dance with her. Then she told me to stay where I was and she went off and found me a pretty young one. We had a ball sort of skipping around together. This is really something too as the tribespeople are very moral and there would never be any question of having an affair with one of their women (unlike the Vietnamese). So to let you dance with one of the wives and one of the girls is an expression of trust and friendliness. While I was out there I took many pictures and bought for almost nothing a terrific Djarai pipe and drinking gourd. I discovered that these people do have some art. It consists of primitive wooden sculptures which are posted on fences around their tombs.... I guess to ward off evil spirits.

After returning from the ceremonies at Plei Mrong, I went to the officers' lounge at the MAAG compound. Had I not been so hyped and my mind so full of the day's events, I would have stopped first at the office and secured my 38 pistol. But I didn't think of that and it remained holstered on my hip. At the bar, I was having a beer with a couple of guys giving an account of the dedication of the Plei Mrong Special Forces camp when a good-looking young American woman entered the room and started asking questions. She was a reporter from the *New York Times* and the only American woman I ever saw in Pleiku. She said how disappointed she was at having missed going to the dedication at Plei Mrong, especially when she heard that Neil Sheehan of *Newsweek* had been there. Scoop lost, apparently. At one point, she asked to have a look at my pistol and—anything to impress a girl—I removed it from the holster and showed it to her. Not cool.

Rob Kuhn, who was present and watching, jumped up and took the weapon, unloaded it, and strode out of the room. I stayed. Clearly, the reporter was relishing the attention she was getting from the officers. When someone suggested she should check out the nightlife in Pleiku, we all took off in various vehicles to the Blue Spring Bar downtown and there the party continued. One member of the group was MAAG's deputy commander, a lieutenant colonel. Despite my "civilian" status, I was sufficiently aware of the rule of rank to stay at the outskirts of the social scene, especially as he monopolized conversation with Ms. *New York Times*. The party was still going on when, finally, I ran out of fuel and drove myself back to the office and collapsed in bed. End of story? Not quite.

The next morning, I awoke late with a stinking hangover to find Rob Kuhn pacing the room in a fierce temper. He let me know I had been way out of line bringing a loaded weapon into the officers' lounge, and I had no business running after a woman the second in command was pursuing. As the saying goes, I got royally chewed up one side and down the other. And, of course, he was right, at least about the weapon—an oversight, sorry, won't happen again. As to the rest, I told him he was distorting the facts and was full of shit and I'd talk to whomever I damn well pleased and hadn't even spoken with the lady in question when we went downtown. Kuhn would accept no defense and informed me that he had already been to II Corps headquarters and apologized in person to the colonel about my behavior. At that point I realized I had a real problem: Rob thought he had something on me and he was going to take full advantage. He had pulled himself out of his alcoholic torpor and was going to play his bust-the-Yalie card. So I wasn't surprised when he drove to the airport and caught the afternoon mail run to Saigon. Things quieted down in the Pleiku Field Office. Finding myself alone, I caught up on sleep.

I wondered, of course, just what his game would be. Get an Article 15 (a non-judicial punishment that commanders use to promote good order and discipline) on my record? But that would be Gallagher's call, not his. Initially, I had that oh-boy-am I-ever-in-trouble-now anxiety in the pit of my stomach. Then, I thought, what the hell, let's play this out—it could prove interesting. Coming up with some disciplinary action will give the Saigon office crowd something to talk about. Behavior unbecoming a private first class? The whole matter seemed ludicrous and I thought that whatever they put in my 201 file would be fine, for I had no intention of staying in the army as a career. On the other hand, I did have some pride and personal honor at stake and an instinct for self-defense. So my attitude shifted from worry to disdain to defense to bring-it-on. I was the only agent working in the field north of Saigon and sending in reports. I figured if there was a problem, well, they would learn about Kuhn's descent into alcoholism!

For three days Rob was gone during which I heard nothing. Then one day he walked into the room, said hello, and, to my surprise, acted as sweet and mild as a pussycat. He was silent about the incident and offered not a word about what he did in Saigon. Nor was there mention of a reprimand. Life picked up as normal. Except, he quit drinking (at least for a while) and never again gave me trouble.

While Rob was away, my friend at headquarters sent up the forms to be completed for a field commission. His note said I'd be a shoo-in to make lieutenant if Gallagher received the paperwork before he left. The whole business confused me—I'd thought I was up for disciplinary action and now was being advised to apply for a commission? Whatever. I filled out the application and was about to put it in the mail when I learned that as an officer my reserve status would change. As I wrote home, "[I would] *run a little more of a chance of letting the Army interfere with my life in the future if there should (as there probably will) be enkindled more military conflagrations requiring the recall of trained reservists. I am already desirable enough with my training and experience without asking for trouble by being an officer to boot.*" I tore up the form.

Excerpt from a letter to my parents dated January 10, 1963:

Enclosed is a "letter of commendation" sent to me by Major Gallagher, my ex-commander. He returned "stateside" last week. He is an extremist—a man who sees things in black & white and who gets carried away by his own eloquence (or oratory) with the result that a good or bad thing gets blown up out of proportion. A letter of commendation is given by a commander to certain individuals under his command who have exhibited outstanding performance in the line of duty.

143

Part II

Gallagher, now a lieutenant colonel (he'd received a promotion), had written the Letter of Commendation shortly before Kuhn turned up in Saigon—presumably with the objective of having me disciplined. As I imagined the scene, the commander had listened to Kuhn's complaint, and then, true-to-form, had a tantrum and turned the tables on the master sergeant.

ASGV-ASC—27 December 1962

SUBJECT: Letter of Commendation
TO: Private First Class David G. Noble
RA 11 399 340
704th INTC Detachment (CI)
APO 143, San Francisco, California

Upon the occasion of my relinquishing command of this detachment, incident upon my return to CONUS, I wish to commend you for the truly outstanding manner in which you have performed your assigned duties in this detachment during the period from 12 May 1962 to 27 December 1962.

Because you are a mature, level-headed, persevering and conscientious individual, the assignments levied upon you have been sensitive, demanding, and heavy. You have been required to operate for long periods of time on your own without direct supervision. Your fine educational background, native intelligence, linguistic abilities, resourcefulness and untiring efforts have enabled you to produce consistently outstanding results. You have always been more than equal to the challenges you have faced. Your courteous, well-bred manner and your good humor have made you well liked and respected by your peers and your superiors alike.

You may take justifiable pride in the fact that you have contributed greatly to the mission success enjoyed by this unit. You have been a distinct credit to yourself, to this detachment and to the United States Army. You have my personal gratitude for a job well done. I wish you continued success in the future.

A copy of this letter will be placed in your Field 201 File as a matter of permanent record.

GORDON S. GALLAGHER
Major—AIS
Commanding

Plei Mrong
Is Attacked

On January 3, less than two weeks after its dedication ceremony, disaster struck the hamlet and Special Forces camp at Plei Mrong. Misled by falsely planted intelligence indicating that a large Viet Cong force was operating in another location in the area, members of our Special Forces team led a force of Bahnar irregulars they had been training on a multi-day patrol to find and engage the enemy.

The leader of this Viet Cong force was an individual from North Vietnam who had already gained considerable notoriety. The passage of time has deleted his name from my memory, so I'll refer to him simply as X. By all reports, he was charismatic, multilingual, and a brilliant tactician who treated the Montagnards as equals and won their admiration and allegiance. He had recruited and trained a loyal following and also developed an effective intelligence network. To blend into the native population, he used a variety of disguises. There were stories about his feats, some no doubt exaggerated if not invented, such that he had become a kind of folk hero in the region. One story going around told of him, disguised as an old man, encountering an ARVN patrol on a trail. When the soldiers asked him if he knew where they could find X, he sent them off on a wild goose chase. Given their feelings toward the Vietnamese and ARVN, the Montagnards delighted in such stories. Vietnamese army patrols were forever chasing this wily, elusive figure, but he was never captured, at least not while I was in the country. One Special Forces sergeant at Plei Mrong I knew became obsessed with tracking this VC commander down and killing him; it became his personal and constantly unfulfilled mission.

With Plei Mrong's best-trained men away, only inexperienced Jarai trainees and a handful of American Green Berets were left to defend the camp and hamlet. At 2:00 a.m. on January 3, two Viet Cong companies led by X attacked and overran the camp. Apparently, the camp's Montagnard strike force already had been infiltrated by Viet Cong, and the sergeant on duty, who was either a sympathizer or was coerced into collaborating, had issued blank ammunition, or no ammunition, to the young trainees on duty; as a result, more than thirty of these young Montagnards were killed. The Green Berets and their Montagnard soldiers were hard to reach but finally notified about the attack on the Plei Mrong camp and when they came back the next day, they found the dead laid out on the ground, the camp's defenses destroyed, many rifles and much ammunition taken, homes burned, the village in shambles, and villagers kidnapped. It was a terrible tragedy, and more than that—a humiliating defeat for II Corps, a warning to the natives, and a setback for the Strategic Hamlet Program. It also proved that Pleiku Province was far from secure and the Viet Cong could operate with impunity within a short distance of II Corps Headquarters. For this to happen in January of 1963 was a shock, and my optimism about winning the war began to dissolve.

Another excerpt from the January 10 letter to my parents:

> ... Remember my last letter describing my day at Plei Mrong village and the rice wine and sacrificial ceremony? ... Well, last Wednesday at 2:00 a.m. it was attacked by two companies (about 400) of Viet Cong. 30 of our troops were killed, 30 wounded and 27 captured or deserted. One US sergeant was slightly injured. The battle lasted four and a half hours—a real slaughter and great morale set-back.

The day after the attack, a number of Montagnards, believed to be ringleaders in the plot to destroy Plei Mrong, were seized, one thought to be a mistress of X, who reputedly had numerous girlfriends in the native villages. These suspects were brought to Pleiku, and Rob Kuhn and I were summoned to participate in an urgently arranged meeting about what to do with the prisoners. In attendance were representatives from our embassy in Saigon, the CIA, and MAAG, G-2. We all felt a strong sense of urgency. We needed to know just what had happened and if a follow-up attack on Plei Mrong or some other village in the vicinity was about to occur. Since this seemed likely, we agreed it was critical to interrogate the Viet Cong suspects quickly.

The immediate question was who would do the interrogating. Although obtaining intelligence was basically a military matter, there was a political dimension as well. This was (still) South Vietnam's war, but Plei Mrong had an American Special Forces camp and training program. There was an assumption among most of the meeting's participants—it seemed likely to me, as well—that if ARVN or a provincial agency handled the POW interrogations, the results would be sanitized and we Americans would benefit little.

During the discussion, I maintained a low profile in the back of the room and kept quiet, unsure as to what extent counterintelligence was involved. I should have known better. The Plei Mrong defeat involved espionage and sabotage—of course, this was, indeed, a counterintelligence matter. Being so inexperienced, I had no desire to be involved in POW interrogations. At Fort Holabird, we students had practiced interview techniques with uncooperative subjects whose parts were played by Baltimore professional actors. But interrogating Viet Cong? That had not been in the curriculum.

At one point late in the evening, Rob, who was now sober and recovered from his shakes, stood up and offered our services. I froze as he told the group that his agent, David Noble, had developed such good working relationships with local intelligence and police agencies that if they conducted the interrogations they would certainly share the results with him—me. That seemed to solve the problem, all nodded in approval, and there was a palpable sense of relief. With one exception, for I knew that however good my relations were with people in some Vietnamese agencies, the Plei Mrong disaster was too fraught with politics for anyone to share honest interrogation results. If shared at all, they would be redacted or sanitized. Rob himself had hardly met any of my contacts, and here he was assuring people from the embassy and the CIA that I would have their full cooperation. When he sat down, it was agreed to follow his plan: the Vietnamese would conduct the interrogations and give me a copy of the results.

A feeling of panic swept over me. Without thinking, I found myself standing up and contradicting my boss. Yes, I agreed, I had developed good relations with various agencies, but no, in this situation, I did not expect any of them to share interrogation results quickly, or completely, if at all. There simply was too much at stake and too much military and political face to save. No one would want to accept blame for what had happened at Plei Mrong.

And so, the discussion continued late into the night. In the end, it was decided that Rob and I would conduct the interrogations ourselves with representatives of both ARVN and certain provincial agencies present; that way, everyone would be in on it. The Chief of Province would even provide his own Vietnamese-to-Jarai interpreter. Back at our office, Rob got on the phone with Saigon headquarters and was instructed that the interrogations be written up verbatim, in question-answer format.

Rob and I showed up first thing the next morning at one of the ARVN buildings at II Corps where the interrogations were to be held. Squatting on the ground outside were the captives—sullen, their wrists tied behind their backs with string. We went inside and found the first prisoner to be interrogated already seated by a small table, a guard behind him and wires tied to his thumbs leading to a field telephone on the table. At another table sat two interpreters: French to Vietnamese and Vietnamese to Jarai. Kuhn, in his element now, quickly took charge; this would not be one of Noble's congenial downtown sessions over tea with Captain Bang, Lieutenant Cuong, or the police chief.

The first day went like this: Rob would ask a question, I would translate it into French, an interpreter would retranslate it into Vietnamese, and a third interpreter would put the question into Jarai. The answer would then travel back through the languages in reverse order. So, from start to finish, the sequence was English to French to Vietnamese to Jarai to Vietnamese to French and finally back to English. In the course of this time-consuming

Viet Cong prisoners of war who were suspected of aiding the Viet Cong in the January 1963 attack on Plei Mrong.

148

exercise, two problems arose, one linguistic, the other cultural. All too frequently, the answer I translated back into English hardly related to Rob's original question. And if it did, it was often expressed in a way that was useless, at least to us. But first, the matter of cooperation.

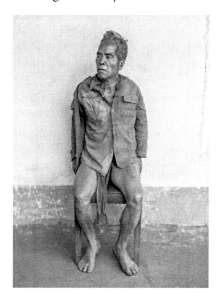

When a prisoner resisted answering a question, the field telephone came into play. I had never even seen a field telephone before, but Rob had, and knew the procedure. When an answer was not forthcoming, he would nod to an ARVN soldier, who would crank its handle to generate an electric charge. When doing this produced responses, he began to use it more liberally. The Vietnamese in the room had set up this method of

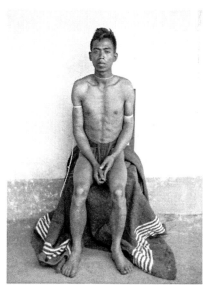

Three Viet Cong suspects believed to be ringleaders in the Plei Mrong attack during which more than 30 young Jarai trainees were killed. They wait to be interrogated.

coercion before we had even showed up, and I realized it was their standard operating procedure. I recalled the final sentence of police interrogation reports I had photocopied in Saigon—"Subject died of natural causes." Compared to that, this was very low-level torture. Still, I questioned its efficacy, and during a break suggested to Rob that the prisoners might be inventing answers in order to stop being shocked. He didn't agree. So it was crank and talk, crank and talk.

On the second day, when the interrogation room was empty during a break, I decided to see what this electric current felt like, and I attached the wires to my own thumbs. Then I reached for the handle. I knew it was low voltage because after turning the handle, the prisoners only twitched or flinched. None fainted, none cried out; none appeared to be in pain. The thing is, when it comes to electricity and electric shocks, I'm chicken. Totally. When I took hold of the handle, I felt the fear and did not crank it. So, would I talk? I thought, maybe. Or maybe I'd see it wasn't so bad. Or maybe I'd find it was worse than it looked. Fact is, I didn't know. Nor did I know what I'd do. Just say my name, rank, and serial number? Or, like a well-trained soldier, make up stuff to mislead the enemy? Or would I tell all?

Some of the captives we were dealing with, it was clear to me, were very tough men. After what they had experienced in their lives and in war, I suspected that a few jolts from a field telephone would be nothing. I also thought that intelligence acquired in this manner would be unreliable. Besides, we already knew that there was a large enemy force out there, flush with victory and now strengthened by a trove of captured American weapons. Would there be another attack? Of course there would be. But where and when? These Montagnard captives probably would not know. Still, *we* needed to know, and quickly. So on we went. Torture has been employed in warfare for centuries, probably millennia, and the issue of whether what we now call "enhanced interrogation" produces useful information continues to plague us. In this case—at least in my own view—there was no "ticking time bomb"; on the contrary, we were caught up in an evolving situation in a slowly progressing conflict.

The prisoners waiting to be interrogated were hunkered down against a cement wall outside the building. Observing them as they waited, I knew they must be wondering what their fate would be. I went out during a break to photograph them, and I jotted down some of their names on a slip of paper: Bet, Dlin, Gru, Nay, Krah, Kreh, Nhor, Lac. Today, nearly sixty years have passed, and I still have that slip of paper with the seven names scrawled on it. A reminder of a bad time.

By day three, Rob had wearied of the process and turned the interrogations entirely over to me. He stayed in the office. I was a complete novice in the business. Interpreting I could do, but trying to squeeze information from battle-hardened Viet Cong? For that I was unprepared. At first, despite my reservations, I did employ the field telephone a couple of times, or just reached for it, but then I put it aside. There were other problems. One was cultural. Concepts that were routine to us, such as direction, time, and location, did not translate well into Jarai and were not well understood. Questions relating to these concepts elicited answers that were meaningless to a person of a different culture. In an intelligence report, some answers came through as absurd. I remember asking one prisoner, for example, for the location of a Viet Cong training camp that we knew was operating somewhere in the area beneath forest canopy. This fellow knew perfectly well where it was; in fact, he had been to it. I asked him how to get there, for directions. What I needed were cardinal references from a known point on a map and distances given in commonly known measurements such as kilometers or walking time. But such concepts were not part of Jarai culture. What I did get were directions in Jarai terms, which included subtle landmarks along a trail from the man's home, wherever that was—markers that were clear and obvious to him but meaningless to the United States Army.

In one session, when I asked the Jarai woman who was believed to be X's mistress when she had last seen him, she held her hand a certain distance above the floor and answered that it was when the rice was so high. Headquarters wanted questions and answers? Well, it got them.

I remember asking another prisoner if he was a "communist." The Vietnamese-to-Jarai interpreter stopped and answered it himself: "Sir, there is no word in the Jarai language for *communist*." I asked how the prisoner felt about "democracy." Also untranslatable. About Ho Chi Minh. The prisoner had never heard of him. Ngo Dinh Diem. Same. These questions were outside the boundaries of their knowledge, culture, and experience. Here we were supposedly fighting to bolster Diem and democracy and trying to defeat communism, and I was learning that Plei Mrong had been laid waste by people who had no words in their language for such concepts and did not even know the names of the presidents of the two Vietnams. Mr. McNamara, put this in your equations.

Each night I would type up an account of the day's interrogations word for word. Early the next morning Rob would drive to the airfield and send my report on a flight to Saigon. Soon I found myself taking perverse satisfaction in the uselessness of what I wrote up. Words such as futility and absurdity entered my mind—about the interrogations, and about everything else. The exercise I was engaged in had become a metaphor of something larger, but not yet clearly defined.

Although I learned some details about the Plei Mrong attack, the more significant information I gained through the interrogations was political. I had asked about the Viet Cong leader I call X, and learned that this figure, so feared and loathed by the Vietnamese and Americans, had achieved near mythic status among the Montagnards. At best, the natives were ambivalent in their loyalties, which made it possible for the Viet Cong to operate with impunity in the countryside.

What I learned from the captives put the Strategic Hamlet Program (also known as the Strategic Village Plan—the great hope for gaining critical control of the Central Highlands) in an unfavorable light. It also threw into question the general state of security within Pleiku Province and the loyalty of the indigenous tribes to the provincial and central governments. In 1963, this should have been useful intelligence, for it challenged the conventional wisdom that the people of South Vietnam wanted America to save them from communism and insurgents inspired by North Vietnam. To be sure, this was local ground-level intelligence, but wasn't it also at this level that we lost the war? Was this intelligence put to use? The answer lies in the fact that the war continued for another twelve years.

The training operation at Plei Mrong restarted on March 16. Contrary to expectations, a follow-up attack on the camp did not occur, at least not immediately. But years later, Plei Mrong was attacked again and demolished. An article in the March 23, 1963, issue of the *Saturday Evening Post* contains a detailed account of the 1963 Plei Mrong battle written by Jerry Rose. (It can be accessed at: *http://www.saturdayeveningpost. com/wp-content/flbk/Im_Hit_Im_Hit_Im_Hit/#/1/.*)

Bangkok

Two weeks interrogating Viet Cong suspects every day and writing up reports at night had been stressful and tiring. So, when Saigon headquarters offered me a five-day R & R in Bangkok, I said yes. My flight left from Tan Son Nhut one morning, and hardly were we in the air than I fell asleep. Sometime later I awoke disoriented and tried to remember where I was. Oh yes, en route to Bangkok. I glanced out the window and saw what appeared to be a vast sea of green waves. Waves between Vietnam and Thailand? Then I realized, I was looking down on the vast expanse of Cambodia's forests. There was no visible sign of human habitation.

As in Hong Kong, I caught an air force van to a hotel downtown where R & R personnel stayed. It was an upscale modern high-rise—not my style, but I wasn't about to forage through a big new city for a small quaint local inn. I checked in and got a street map of the city from the front desk.

Bangkok, I discovered, was a teeming, spread-out metropolis about which I knew nothing. I knew no one and was in no mood to play tourist. Public transportation was a puzzle, and unlike Hong Kong and Saigon, neither English nor French was a second language. Therefore, I walked. Walked and wandered and explored the city's maze of lanes, streets, avenues, and byways, checking my map from time to time to avoid getting lost. I walked till my feet ached as I observed street life and got a feel for neighborhoods along the way. What struck me above all else was the poverty: decrepit houses, raggedy begging children, and canals choked with debris and sewage. And everywhere, it seemed, there was noise and traffic.

One morning I visited a beautiful temple complex. In its courtyard, a friendly Thai student struck up a conversation with me in English and accompanied me as I walked around. He tried to explain a little about what I was seeing. When we parted company, he encouraged me to see some "floating gardens," where I could take a ride in a boat through canals and marketplaces. He even offered to be my guide at no charge. Of course, I agreed, and we arranged to meet the day after next at my hotel.

Mother had sent me the name of a silk merchant, James Thompson, who was a friend of her sister. After World War II, Thompson had settled in Thailand and set about reviving Thailand's silk industry. Apparently, he'd been successful, for he had a shop in the city, The Thai Silk Co., Ltd., and an historic house built in classical Thai architectural style in the country where he reputedly kept a priceless art collection. I decided to pay him a visit.

Excerpts from a letter to my parents dated January 25, 1963:

Happy New Year! Today is the first day of the Chinese (Buddhist) new year and it's a big holiday.

I got back from Bangkok last Wednesday and came up from Saigon on Thursday morning. I cut my leave short by 3 days as I was disappointed in Bangkok and wasn't enjoying myself too much.... I saw a couple of splendid temples, walked around the city, went dancing and drinking and stayed at a class A hotel with swimming pool. To my mind, Bangkok was a very tiring city—hard to get around, dirty, impersonal, crowded and not what I was interested in. I didn't have the historical and religious background to appreciate the temples. The language was a big barrier and, of course, I knew no one. I went to see Mr. Thompson at his shop. He is a nice fellow.

I had been trying to get in touch with him unsuccessfully so I went to the store, a small silk shop, and who should I bump into but an old flame named Dede Newton whom I knew at Boston parties ... a very nice girl and pretty. Was I ever surprised! So was she! This was at 4:30 p.m. I immediately made a date with her and figured that if Mr. Thompson or/and she offered the hope of a better 3 days, I'd stay. But Mr. Thompson was quite cool and didn't invite me anywhere. Dede asked me to her house—her father being stationed in Bangkok with the Air Force. I, of course, gave her the old line about the whys, hows, and wheres of my civilian status.

We walked into her house and ... "I'd like to introduce you to my father, General Newton." Which sort of faked me out. I'd had no idea! He's a wheel in SEATO. I'm not supposed to conceal my rank from a general officer nor are generals' daughters supposed to date enlisted men. So it was a slight predicament. I took another look at the daughter and chose the natural course and it all worked out very smoothly.... This was the first American girl I'd spoken to in 9 months. Afterwards, the general went to a social function and Mrs. Newton took [Dede's] baby sister to the movies—terribly thoughtful. I discovered that to be in the jungles of Vietnam is considered by those who only read newspaper reports to be a sort of a heroic position to be in.... P.S. I'm sending a big box of souvenirs home. Feel free to open and look over the things. I'm sure they'll interest you immensely. There are tribal baskets, sabres, guitars, violins, cloth, pipes and Vietnamese plates, Japanese silk and some other dust collectors. Oh yes, also a quiver of Viet Cong poisoned arrows. The poison is supposed to be ineffective after 2 weeks, but better be careful of the tips anyway.

Bangkok

One was analyzed by the FBI lab in Washington with positive results. I couldn't fit my two crossbows in the box.

After Pleiku, all-male messes, and the problems with Rob Kuhn—not to mention the POW interrogations—I really appreciated the warm family atmosphere of the Newton's home.

The following day, Dede had to be at work and she was busy in the evening. So I was on my own. I explored more on foot until weary and thirsty, then I stopped at a bar for a beer. The place was empty, but the bartender assured me that if I came back in the evening, I would be pleasantly surprised. So, I went back later and found the place hopping—music and girls. As usual, I desired female companionship, but on a more basic level than making conversation with a general's daughter. This place had a live band and pretty Thai girls on the make. After a few drinks and dances, I found myself in a cab with one of them headed for her place. When we got there, she led me up a series of wood ramps, then along boardwalks to her house, one of many built on stilts over the water. Already it was an adventure.

Her house was small, two or three rooms, and sparsely furnished. From it I could hear the sound of conversations in nearby dwellings in the lilting tones of the Thai language. She asked me for her fee, about fifteen dollars, which I gave her. It was late by now and we went to bed. She was a little older than I was and exceedingly beautiful with straight glossy black hair that hung below her waist. She was friendly and relaxed, and we talked, as she spoke some English. I couldn't believe my luck. After sex, when she learned I was paying for a hotel room, she urged me to come stay with her. Soon after, she wanted to make love again, for herself, she said. The night was hot and muggy, and as I was drifting off to sleep, she kneeled over me waving a large fan to make a breeze. This night was exactly the kind of relaxing therapy I needed. Vietnam slipped out of my mind and I slept soundly.

In the morning, we made love once more. Soon afterward, a neighbor came by to sell her some food. She pulled a bankroll out from under the mattress to pay for it, and I saw on top the dollars I'd given her the night before. She then went out to do an errand. While she was gone, on a sudden impulse, I reached under the mattress and took back the money I'd paid her.

Why I did this is something I've never understood—it was an impulse theft. I rationalized that because she had enjoyed the sex so much, why should *I* be paying *her*? Whatever the motivation, it was an unexpected

155

spontaneous act, and no sooner was the deed done than I wanted to undo it. But too late; she returned. I felt panic, hurriedly dressed, and over her protests said I had to go.

I went back along the boardwalks and ramps and found myself on a busy street, where I hailed a cab. As we started off, the woman I'd been with, who had treated me so well appeared next to the vehicle. She asked why I'd taken back the money, saying she was poor. But already the cab had started moving through traffic. I was in disbelief over what had happened and had a new image of myself—a thief. I went over and over it in my mind but did not understand.

I checked out of the hotel and found a small modest one that didn't cater to soldiers and tourists. That evening I had a Thai meal that nearly scorched the skin off my tongue. Punishment already! Early the next morning I got on a flight back to Saigon. So, that was it for Bangkok. It was a crazy time. One craziness leads to another.

Excerpt from a letter to my parents dated February 11, 1963:

> *I got all your birthday cards.... Also* [one] *from the general's daughter in Thailand—amazing! She asked me my birthday and sent a card. 24 now—each year is smaller in relation to my past life. This year was only 1/24th of my life; ten years ago it was 1/14th. So, in a sense, this was the least significant year of my life. But that's a foolish criterion ... actually it was a pretty original and different year.*

Excerpt from a letter to George Hobson dated February 18, 1963:

> *Oh, I didn't mention Bangkok. I spent a few days there last month. Actually I didn't have a terribly good time. It is a very hard city to cope with as a foreigner who arrives cold. I did a little sightseeing and hell-raising but did not really have much spirit while I was there. I had been working very hard for a couple of weeks at a nasty business ... interrogations of prisoners of war. What I really wanted was to relax, to meet someone nice and have a change. So I ended up rather lonely.*

Ban Me Thuot

Letter to my parents dated about February 11, 1963:

... I'm going down to Ban Me Thuot in Darlac [Dak Lak] *Province in two days to work on what appears to be an interesting case. I'd like to spend several days there. It's a larger town than Pleiku and it's in Rhadé country. The Rhadé are the largest and most civilized tribe ... most advanced culture. (I'll be flying down) We had a major killed here last week when his bomber crashed. The other American and Vietnamese bailed out and were rescued. I saw them bring the American in by chopper after 3 days lost in the jungle. Boy, did he ever look happy!*

Did I write you that I met Ambassador Nolting in Saigon last month? Yesterday he and his family came to Pleiku to dedicate a new American surgical hospital. Like a fool I didn't attend. As it turned out I would have had a chance to talk with him—usually this doesn't happen with dignitaries.

Excerpt from a letter to George H. Hobson dated February 18, 1963:

The dry season is in full swing now. The ground is parched and the wind carries the red dust into everything. The nights are cool and the days warm ... similar to a New England October or September. Next April the rains will begin and by June this red dirt will turn to black mud and the countryside to a swamp. The average yearly rainfall is about 150 inches. Two years ago there were 180 inches ... that makes well over an inch a day ... fantastic! I'm glad I'll not be around as it must get really gloomy.

I went to Ban Me Thuot several times on assignments or as a stopover en route to some other place. I liked the city, which was the capital of Dak Lak Province, and sometimes stayed in a small hotel on the main street away from the MAAG compound and its unwelcoming commanding officer. It had cafés and bars and dusty streets, and native Rhadé tribespeople trekked into town from the hinterlands to trade. To me, it had the feel of an old western town in America, at least as so often depicted in movies.

One matter I was to investigate concerned sightings of a tall blond Westerner who was reported leading a band of Viet Cong guerrillas in the region. Could he be an American? As I had no native contacts in the town, no interpreter, and no way to get around, this job presented a challenge and, in the end, I was never able learn much about him or who he was. My best guess was that he was a former French legionnaire who'd been captured by the Viet Minh years before, gone native, and found a new role with the Viet Cong.

In Ban Me Thuot there existed a covert American military intelligence outfit known as Field Operations Intelligence (FOI). Their role involved the collection of *positive*, rather than *counter*, intelligence. Of course, that was mostly what I was doing, too. Marco Einaudi, the agent who had loaned me his Land Rover, was with them and based in Ban Me Thuot, although he spent time in Pleiku, as well. He had provided me an introduction to his colleagues, who had a house in the town.

One afternoon, one of the FOI agents invited me to join him for a couple of beers at a bar he frequented in town. It was a small cozy place owned and run by an Indian-Vietnamese woman who had South Vietnamese citizenship. While we were chatting with her, her husband came in, a Frenchman with whom my companion also was acquainted. Pierre—I'll call him Pierre for my gnome's Ban Me Thuot drawer is missing that note—was a jolly well-fed character with dark bushy hair who, like Claude in Pleiku, was delighted to meet an American who spoke his tongue. He was a French citizen but, by being married to a Vietnamese citizen, could legally co-own real estate, and he had a plantation—rubber or coffee—outside of Ban Me Thuot. As I recall, it had belonged to him before the enactment of property reforms after 1954 and now, through his marriage, he was able to hold onto it. Perhaps it was a *marriage de convenance*, but whatever their personal relationship, he told me enthusiastically about his place and urged us to come out for dinner the following evening. For us, he said, he would roast not the fatted calf but a wild boar. It was hard to say no, and I didn't.

Pierre's plantation was off in the boondocks, quite a distance from town. The area was "insecure," a euphemism for Viet Cong infested, and the prospect of driving out there gave me some pause. On the other hand, it was a good bet that Central Registry knew little about French planters and now I had a chance to learn something that could, in Mr. Gallagher's words, "assist General Harkins' efforts in Southeast Asia." Besides, where was there a secure area? As a precaution, I left my CIC credentials behind. This left me with no identification at all for I had long before been relieved of my dog tags. If taken prisoner…. Well, not something to think about.

For the first leg of the trip, we drove on a well-traveled paved road.

After some kilometers, we turned onto a single-lane dirt road that headed deep into the forest, and from that we branched onto a narrow track leading to the plantation. It was dusk when we arrived at Pierre's log cabin, situated at the edge of a clearing beyond which lay farmland and orchards. Pierre lived here by himself. His operation, I observed, was a far cry from the Catecka Plantation. Kerosene lanterns and candles illuminated the rustic interior of his simple abode with its spare furnishings, and I felt as if I were on a frontier of sorts. In fact, being there reminded me of the summer I had lived and worked on a small cattle ranch in British Columbia's interior in 1955.

Pierre was an attentive host and, to my surprise, produced a bottle of whiskey. This got us all off to a good start while his houseboy finished preparing dinner. His plantation manager, another Frenchman, also was present. As we drank, the aromas of roasting pig spread into the cabin from his small kitchen. When it came time to eat, we drew around the dining table and watched while Pierre brought out a sizzling platter of wild boar—just shot by his Montagnard workers—along with roast potatoes and a bottle of very passable French wine.

Pierre was one of the few French colonists from the earlier period who had been able to carry on as before in the countryside, a testament to his powers of adaptation. Now, of course, he had to deal not only with the government but with the Viet Cong, who, he said—and I noted with some apprehension—regularly came through the plantation. He had worked out his own accord with them: he simply paid them off, a cost of doing business. In return, they let him and his workers go about their work. It was a win-win for all. Other than trips to town to obtain supplies and see his woman—it had been on one of these that I met him—Pierre led quite a hermetic life, interacting mostly with his Montagnard workers. The reclusive, hard-working lifestyle seemed to appeal to him.

That evening, we had a rousing good time storytelling, laughing, stuffing our bellies, and reducing Pierre's stock of red wine. The hours slid by, however, and as it grew later and later, I began to grow uneasy over the prospect of retracing the route back to town. Roads never look quite the same in the dark, especially going the other way, and I worried about our possibly taking a wrong turn, getting lost, being intercepted, and so forth. But these were fleeting concerns, for the conversation and Pierre's supply of wine assuaged my anxieties.

We got drunk, and it was very late when we finally left the conviviality of the cabin. As we drove through the enclosing forest, only a small bobbing pool of light from the jeep's headlights warded off the intense darkness around us. My companion drove fast, too fast I thought, but maybe not fast enough, while I peered ahead anticipating a "roadblock" every time we went around a bend in the narrow road. I worried that every bump might be a land mine. Enclosed by the trees and the darkness, I also thought: what idiots we are! We should not be here, where are we? But my friend conveyed confidence, and as each kilometer ticked off, my concerns eased until, finally, we reached the highway and I felt safe again. Before long, the lights of town greeted us.

Excerpt from a letter to my parents dated February 19, 1963:

... I have spent the past five days in Ban Me Thuot, a city of the southern Haut Plateau, staying with some fellows in an agency similar to mine. Had a really great time. As it turned out I had very little work to do, so it turned out to be sort of a vacation. I met a number of French planters who manage or own coffee and rubber plantations in the vicinity. This was interesting. I like the French in some respects and dislike them in others. They seem to be a very opinionated and arrogant bunch, but taken with a grain of salt, they are very amusing and expressive, and I enjoy practicing my French and learning their "argot." I'm so glad for my being able to speak French. Over here it is uncommon for an American and so makes it easy to make foreign friends who don't speak English. These French are a weird crowd. They are the dregs of the French Empire who have not wanted to return. As far as I'm concerned, anyone who would choose to remain in this country must have a pretty damned good reason for not going home. And most of them do. Either they ran into big trouble in France and sought refuge in Indo China long ago, or they were adventurers and scoundrels in the Foreign Legion who deserted when the chips were down. They have free travel throughout the country since the VC don't bother with them except to tax the plantations. Many of them have very colorful and unusual pasts.

Excerpt from a letter to my brother and sister-in-law, February 18, 1963:

... I've just been spending 5 days in Ban Me Thuot, in the southern High Plateau region. This is a significant city in SVN, but only a town by our standards ... no, I take that back; population-wise it is a true city. But being so compact and crowded (30,000–40,000) and slummy, it seems like a town. There are quite a number of French coffee and rubber plantations in the area. I visited one of these (at night) and ate a dinner of roast wild boar over candlelight and "vin rouge." I was with two fellow cloak-and-dagger types, and our hosts were two French planters who have been here for many years. We had a very gay evening drinking Scotch, and the "last ones for the road" (12 kms. through the jungle) lasted until very late and I didn't get to bed until 3:00 a.m. The following night some French and metises (½ & ½) girls and another French planter came over to the villa I am living in and we sat up drinking, singing and dancing till 3:00 a.m. I've had a very good time, had a change from Pleiku, and seen a glimpse of another side of Vietnamese life (i.e. French plantations)....

[The French] have virtual freedom of movement within the country now. The VC do not touch them. I do not like them [the French] on the whole. They tend to be a very opinionated bunch of loudmouths who sneer and snicker at Americans for wasting their time on these dirty "peaux de citrons" (lemon skins) and laugh at us because of the economic merry-go-round which winds up with corrupt Vietnamese officials pocketing 50% of U.S. aid. For people from a sorry washed-up country, they sure are arrogant. As far as I'm concerned they're all bark and no bite, and for them to argue with Americans is like a flea-bitten mongrel yapping at a Great Dane. But I will agree with them that the Vietnamese are not in themselves worth fighting for. The cause, yes, but after dealing with these people for only a year, it's evident that their cultural, moral and material standards are far below ours, and they do not deserve all the aid they are receiving. And they realize the Americans are not here out of charity and so spend lots of energy trying to cover up their inferiority ... face saving. (The above opinions probably sound wrong to you, but they are the result of my contact with Vietnamese. I don't like them and I don't respect them and so I don't like seeing them freeload off the U.S. and our wealth and experience and genius which took us many years and wars to develop.)

Today, more than half a century on, I have no recollection of thinking this way about the French and Vietnamese I met over there. What I remember is liking them and enjoying their company and appreciating the friendliness and hospitality they showed me. It's hard to explain this contradiction except to say that such is memory. My wizened little gnome is not such a wizard, after all—he's a trickster. But such too is maturity— there's a deep gulf between being twenty-three and eighty-one. Another possibility is that when I was penning those letters, other things were angering me and I was just venting steam; or, after eight months in the army in Vietnam, I had simply begun to acquire "an attitude."

There was another matter I heard about while in Ban Me Thuot and it was something I wanted to investigate, although I had little notion how to go about it. It concerned reports that a French-Cambodian woman was making trips back and forth between the highlands of Vietnam and Cambodia with the objective of reviving a long-existing Montagnard autonomy movement among the Rhadé. What I had heard was that she crossed the border and traveled through this remote region by elephant. The tribal groups extended across borders—Vietnam, Laos, Cambodia, Thailand—and although they spoke different languages, they shared many cultural traits, followed a similar way of life, and for a long time had experienced oppression by both the Vietnamese and French. I knew very little about Vietnam's history or Vietnamese-French-Montagnard relations while I was in Pleiku. Later, however, I learned through reading books by Bernard Fall and Gerald Cannon Hickey that, under French rule, the vast mountainous tribal region had been set aside by France as a Crown Domain under Emperor Bao Dai and a Vietnamese person needed good reason to enter Montagnard country. (The impressive MAAG compound in Ban Me Thuot, where I had first stayed, had been built by Bao Dai as his hunting lodge.) Both the French and Bao Dai had offered the Montagnards autonomy. After Ngo Dinh Diem became president in 1955, however, this policy was abandoned, and the new Republic of Vietnam wanted to develop the highlands economically by resettling lowland Vietnamese there and assimilating the Montagnards into Vietnamese culture. This was the catalyst for a nationalistic movement to grow among the mountain tribes with the goal of regaining control of appropriated land and achieving autonomy.

Since their lands accounted for two thirds of the country, control of this large territory was critical to winning the war. All sides—North Vietnam, South Vietnam, the National Liberation Front (Viet Cong), and the Americans—desired the support of the Montagnards and tried to gain it by either friendly or coercive means. The South Vietnam government knew it needed the mountain tribes on its side against the growing Viet Cong threat but, understandably, had reservations about American Special Forces arming the Montagnards with rifles and training them in their use. The government's plan was to retrieve the weapons after winning the war. Of course, that was not to be.

This woman who was supposedly trying to revitalize the Montagnard Liberation Movement was reputedly a former airline flight attendant, the current mistress of a high Cambodian official, and beautiful. It all seemed very intriguing, straight out of an Ian Fleming spy novel. But on the serious side, it also seemed important, for a Montagnard rebellion in the Highlands had the potential to destabilize the fragile Diem regime, sway the course of the war, and have significant implications for the United States.

But how to find out more? Of course, I knew what James Bond would do—meet this alluring female in a swank bar over a martini. Well, I had been to a bar, but all I'd gotten was an invitation to sup on roast pig with a French farmer. Realistically, not speaking Rhadé and having no interpreter or transportation, it was clear this assignment was beyond my abilities and I called it quits. Still, I reported the little I knew, and soon after got the impression that it made a stir in Saigon headquarters.

While in Ban Me Thuot, I did stumble upon a more prosaic situation that lined up with my CIC training. While having dinner with my FOI colleagues at their house in town, I noticed that, despite the supposedly highly covert nature of their operation, they functioned in a remarkably lax fashion. The senior officer, an informal laid-back captain, gave me a friendly welcome, probably assuming I was an officer as well. Everyone ate together and, in contrast to conditions at Central Registry in Saigon, he was on casual social terms with his subordinates. When we sat down to eat, a local Vietnamese woman joined us at the table. As dinner progressed, I realized that she was the captain's girlfriend. What was more, he drank a lot and had a loose tongue. The situation made me increasingly uncomfortable, and I didn't know quite what to do. I seemed to be party to a significant and ongoing breach of security. The captain knew that I was CIC and that military security was central to the CIC's mission. Had Gallagher been present, he would have had a stroke. For me, however, as a lower-ranking counterintelligence agent, taking this officer aside and reading him the riot act—well, it didn't seem like a realistic option. So what did I do? At the end of the meal, I excused myself and left.

Upon returning to Pleiku, I described the situation to Rob Kuhn and asked his advice. He mulled it over, and then agreed I had witnessed a security problem and should report it, which I did. If Saigon wanted it investigated, Rob would be just the guy to do it. He could be a tough, imposing, no-nonsense figure and was about ten years senior to the FOI officer. I recalled what he told me when I first met him—he wouldn't take any shit from anyone without first busting his head. No junior captain was about to intimidate this seasoned master sergeant.

Before leaving Vietnam, I knew of no follow-up on this matter; however, not long after arriving at my next duty station, in White Plains, New York, I got a call from a CIC agent in the New York City headquarters who wanted to interview me. He came to White Plains, put me under oath, and asked me to give an account of the Ban Me Thuot situation. Saigon, it seemed, had initiated a full background check in connection with reviewing the captain's security clearance. It was a politic way of dealing with a sensitive internal problem.

Final Months
in Pleiku

As U.S. involvement in Vietnam grew, Pleiku's MAAG compound was under constant construction. However, since this was still the "advisor" phase of the war, American soldiers had a very limited direct-combat role. Our military forces were at around the 4,000 level when I had arrived in April 1962, but they were growing rapidly. And by no means was everyone an advisor. I wasn't: Central Registry Detachment had a unilateral mission.

Construction work around MAAG, Pleiku, was contracted out to local builders. I was struck by the division of labor: the masons, all men, laid the bricks and blocks while the women did the heavier manual labor, such as mixing mortar and carrying bricks. They carried these heavy materials on palettes or in buckets that hung from the end of a rod that lay across their shoulders. Under such weight, they had to walk with a short shuffle step. Some of the female workers took their midday break in front of our quarters, where they would sit in a row, back-to-front, picking lice and grooming each other, all the while giggling in merriment. They burst into laughter when I brought out my camera one day and snapped some pictures. This scene came to mind many years later when I attended a lecture by Jane Goodall and saw pictures of chimps engaged in the same activity. Apparently nitpicking goes far back in our common primate history!

President Diem himself came to Pleiku toward the end of my time there. As when General Dinh entered Ban Me Thuot, the locals—Montagnards, Vietnamese, and mobs of schoolchildren—were turned out to line the road that linked the airport to town as they waited for the president's plane to arrive. I went, too, armed with my new Bell & Howell 8mm movie camera, and found a place in the crowd along the road overlooking the airstrip. We waited, and waited, then waited some more. In the midday sun.

Construction laborers picking nits during their lunch break.

A couple of hours went by. Finally, the long-awaited plane came into sight and I began filming. It doglegged around the airport, landed, and a red carpet was rolled out as the doors opened. With what footage I had left, I immortalized the president of South Vietnam stepping out and waving.

But there was a problem: when I zoomed in for a closer shot, the figure deplaning was not Ngo Dinh Diem—it was his second. This was a test, only a test, I was told—when the real Diem arrives, you will be notified. By then, however, I was out of patience and out of film, and returned to the office. Later in the day, Diem did arrive. Of course, the peasants and children remained huddled in groups along the road waiting for their choreographed moment to stand and applaud.

As my tour of duty in Vietnam neared completion, I was asked to stay on. Now I was broken in and knew my way around and had formed professional relationships with people in the Highlands. By this time, however, my attitude toward the war and my job had drastically shifted, and I had no wish to continue participating in what I considered a futile and wasteful, not to mention deadly exercise. I wanted out of Vietnam and was counting the days. Shortly before, Saigon had sent two new agents to join Rob Kuhn and me in Pleiku, one of whom, Ed Ketterlinus, was to be my replacement. In contrast to Kuhn, I found him to be one of the nicest individuals I ever met. He arrived with a fresh positive attitude and, like me, soon became keenly interested in the Montagnards. He accompanied me on assignments and at meetings and I introduced him to my contacts. After I left, Ed adopted an orphaned Vietnamese child in Saigon, whom he brought up to Pleiku, where she became a favorite of everyone in the MAAG compound—indeed, she became *la fille du régiment.* Unfortunately, like all the Intelligence agents I had met, save for Marco Einaudi and Captain Nelson, in Saigon, Ed spoke neither Vietnamese nor French. The army, clearly, was still having difficulty finding agents with the appropriate job experience and linguistic ability to function effectively in Southeast Asia. To be sure, the CIC was sending over Niseis; at least in physical appearance, they blended in to the population better than the likes of me.

One Nisei colleague was Warrant Officer James H. Ishihara, from Hawaii, whom we all liked a lot. He had come to Vietnam with the initial contingent and started a field office in the Delta, where, at that time, most of the fighting was going on. Sadly, Jim died from a Viet Cong bullet shortly before his tour ended. Jim was Central Registry's first loss. I later learned that he had served in the highly decorated 442nd Infantry in World War II, the most decorated unit in U.S. military history. Jim was two years older than Senator Daniel Inouye and probably served with him in the 442nd.

Excerpt from a letter to my parents dated March 11, 1963:

> ... We all got some bad news a couple of days ago. Jim Ishihara, our friend and fellow agent, was killed by the communists. He was flying in an airplane and a single bullet hit him in the head. It was the only shot fired and he just keeled over. He was a wonderful guy liked by everyone who knew him ... if only he had sat in another seat. Also, he was going to retire next year from the army and this was his last assignment. It just makes me sick.

Excerpt from a letter to George H. Hobson dated February 18, 1963:

> ... The Vietnamese belong to an unstable, 8-year-old nation most of which does not support the ruling government. They are fighting under the attempted guidance and support of Americans who belong to the oldest democratic nation in the world, who have been strong and stable for generations, who have fought through the greatest wars in history and won and so forth and so on. When the average American goes out on the battlefield, he performs better than the average Vietnamese. This is superiority. I sympathize with these people because they have had it rough. But when you deal with this country and its agencies and compartments,

you are dealing with second-rate stuff. Their politics are corrupt. Their legal system is corrupt. Justice is whom you bribe. Success is whom you know, what family you belong to and what your political beliefs are. This is no criterion for selecting qualified individuals for positions of great responsibility. Of course, if you did not use this system, big Diem ... would be soon cold meat. Diem is the butt of many jests amongst the Americans including myself. Actually, I am sure he is a good man, means well, is smart, educated and so forth. Only he is the most misinformed man in Vietnam and if anyone dares inform him he awaits to be forever lost and forgotten by the world as soon as he has his say. Diem sees and knows only what his underlings show and tell him. To get away from the institutions such as government, law, and military (not to mention religion!) and go into the intangible realms of morality (western), the Vietnamese do not measure up to our standards. O.K., I agree. I'll throw no stones at anyone else's morality if they throw none at mine. If they want to lie in your face with a smile, fine, so long as it is not my face. You see, I really feel strongly about this. But I also understand my feelings and base most of them on facts which I see around me. I am not prejudiced. I came here innocent and open and I gave the Oriental the benefit of many doubts when arguing with my associates. But time and again I am disillusioned.

Excerpt from a letter to my parents dated March 11, 1963:

... We were all disgusted over here by the recent spiteful talk of Madame Nhu, the President's sister-in-law, against the U.S. She is hated by Americans and Vietnamese alike and I just hope someone comes along and assassinates her one of these days. She is really detestable. She knows that the Americans find the Vietnamese people a big disappointment not to mention the regime in power including herself; so her best defense is a cheap offense. Her remarks against the U.S. sound to me just like Communist propaganda. Enclosed is a clipping. America has [lost] 60-odd lives, billions of dollars, prestige and self-respect ... and Nhu would probably herself be in a communist prison camp now if not for us. I really do not think Kennedy should take such official remarks sitting down. After 11 months here I only know one Vietnamese that I would trust [This was Bang] and if Kennedy and Nolting and Harkins do not handle them with an iron hand they will skin us alive and then go communist. Even if we are not in command over here, we have a good right to make certain demands. Nhu is anti–American .... I think that the ruling family here is interested in its own power before the welfare of Vietnam (except probably Diem) and that Nhu is trying to appeal to those many Vietnamese who have learned to dislike and mistrust foreign interests within the country. There's only one cure for her and that's the horsewhip.

I have gotten back 300 feet of color film now and they are really good. Am sending all my slides, movies and photos home today in the mail. What a lot of pictures I have! I am scared to let them out of my possession but have no room for them all in my bag when I leave.

Headquarters in Saigon wanted our field office to relocate into town where we would be closer to the people and agencies that were providing us with information. Ed Ketterlinus and I found a house in Pleiku to rent.

Part II

To me, the move seemed unwise. For one thing, we would be sitting ducks to the Viet Cong and for another, how would being situated in town increase the effectiveness of agents who spoke no known local language? I was doubly glad to be leaving.

A couple of days before I departed, I received a message summoning me personally to appear at the office of the Chief of Province. I had seen this individual at functions but never met him. No topic was mentioned. At the appointed time, I showed up at the provincial headquarters where, following protocol, I was kept waiting by myself for a long time in a large empty room. Finally he strode in and took a seat behind his desk. There was no small talk now, nor was I invited to speak at first. His expression was dark with anger as he launched into a diatribe against the findings of the Plei Mrong massacre. Apparently, my report, or some version of it (I never saw the finished product), had worked its way through the system to this official.

The gist of the governor's rant was that the findings from my interrogations of the Plei Mrong suspects were false and erroneous and gave a distorted impression of security conditions in Pleiku Province. He claimed that everything in my report was invalidated by the torture used to extract the information, which he knew about from his own interpreter who had been present. He accused me of spreading poisonous information about his administration, and then asked what I had to say.

I asked him if there had been a massacre at Plei Mrong. No, he said, and brushed if off as just a passing incident. I realized that in his own account he had sanitized the Plei Mrong tragedy. No wonder he was upset. I did not comment on the torture issue because I knew that the coercive methods Rob Kuhn and I had briefly used were a walk in the garden compared to those he and his henchmen routinely employed.

In any event, my main objective at the meeting was simply to let the man blow off steam and to have it end as quickly as possible. There was nothing to discuss, really, as we both knew the truth; this was a political face-saving ritual; it was part of why I was eager to leave the country. This was the man who had earlier ordered the cutting down of the Catecka tea plantation's fruit orchard and stuck the trees in the ground at a strategic hamlet in order to impress (and mislead) President Ngo Dinh Diem.

In a few days, I would be on a plane home. For all I cared, the governor could report that there was no such village of Plei Mrong in Pleiku Province. There were two wars going on in Vietnam: one fought in the countryside, another on the desks of politicians. Camouflaging reality was a way of life. I had been reading the daily ARVN battlefield reports for months, and there was a joke going around that if you totaled up the reported Viet Cong body counts, the resulting figure would surpass the population of the country. And distorting reality was not limited to the Vietnamese side.

In remembering Vietnam and reading letters written while I was there, I recognize the slow evolution in my attitude toward the war. I arrived in that far-off place with spirit, enthusiasm, and a naïve belief that we were in Vietnam to do good. But I came back home changed: discouraged and cynical. My attitude shifted gradually. It started in Saigon when I met and spent time with Colonel Kumar. Then, as the months rolled by and I learned more, my belief in the cause eroded. I did still feel a sense of pride and patriotism in our opposing the aggressive and ruthless spread of communism, but it became clear that we were not making headway. The Viet Cong were operating all through the country, gaining popular support, and enemy forces and supplies were streaming down the Ho Chi Minh Trail, which ran along Vietnam's border with Laos and Cambodia just west of Pleiku, from North Vietnam. What was more, I was no longer under the illusion that the South Vietnamese government was a struggling democracy; it was just another corrupt dictatorial regime. If the U.S. Army and Department of Defense were putting a positive spin on the military situation, the three main American correspondents in the country—Malcolm Browne, David Halberstam, and Neil Sheehan—were writing more objective reports and informing Americans about negative aspects of how the war was progressing.

The day before I left, I went around to say good-bye to my friends and associates in Pleiku. The only person I felt I really would miss was Captain Bang, as he and I had truly become friends. And perhaps Charlie Long, even though I thought his efforts to change the religion of the Jarai to be as misguided, in its own way, as our interference in Vietnam's civil war. It was just another manifestation of cultural arrogance.

I also had a last tea get-together with the Deputy Chief of Province. We talked politely about the year, and he queried me about when exactly I would be leaving. When I told him, he reflected a moment, then said he would now give me something to write in my final report. He was a Buddhist and, as we all knew, to advance in your career you had to be a Roman Catholic. He told me about Vietnamese politics—the Buddhists, Catholics, Americans, and Viet Cong—and with candor that he considered the situation to be hopeless. He painted a gloomy scenario, but I recognized

169

the truth in it. He expressed opinions that I was beginning to arrive at my-self. His comments were sad, for sure, but in his openness, I felt a hopeful note.

He ended our last meeting by saying, "I tell you these things at last be-cause you're leaving tomorrow. I feel like I'm putting a note in a bottle and tossing it in the sea. Maybe someone will read it." He wished me luck. This report I hand carried to Saigon wondering, in our own political-military environment, what would become of it. One thing I knew about the army's bureaucracy: paperwork does get shuffled along. But to what use? I was reminded of Major Gallagher's comment when I had first shown up in Saigon. The military was committed to this thing, he had said, there was no going back, and we were not to question it.

I flew to Saigon and stayed at headquarters for more than a week waiting for my departure plans to solidify and travel orders to be cut. Central Registry had moved to a spacious compound closer to downtown. Major Gallagher's replacement was a mild-mannered lieutenant colonel who gave me a friendly welcome and light duties. The staff had grown, too, and had turned over such that I knew hardly anyone. One newly arrived lieutenant was editing and retyping one of my field reports and invited me to sign it in person. It was the one I had sent down weeks before concern-ing the possibility of a Montagnard insurgency—the paperwork was shuf-fling along. Normally, my name was typed at the bottom of reports, but they were signed off by someone at headquarters. When I read his edited version, I found that the young officer had misunderstood what I wrote and muddled its meaning. I pointed out the problem and tried to explain the Montagnard situation in the Highlands. The lieutenant was like I had been twelve months before, clueless. He had probably only read the *New Yorker* article my mother had sent.

Sensing my exasperation, he grew defensive and told me to correct and retype the report myself. I did and restored its original meaning. In twelve months, it was the only field report I personally signed.

Excerpts from a letter to my parents dated April 15, 1963:

... I've been in Saigon for 6 days now and have six more before departing. They have me doing clerical work which is pretty dull, but I have most evenings off and a girlfriend downtown. So I'm very glad to be here for my last 12 days in Viet-nam. Saigon is a wonderful city. It's the kind of city one would like to live in if the circumstances were right. I'm certain that under the French domination it was a paradise, as was every city in Vietnam, for the French. Now, it can be fine if you're a civilian working for the State Dept., a business firm, etc. If you have money, a French "villa" and a social circle, you can live in an atmosphere of luxury and

leisure which is only possible to attain, I think, in a country where the standards of living are low and the people poor. Know what I mean? The colonialist way of life must be very attractive ... and as history has shown, hard not to abuse. Look at the French ... thousands and thousands of lives lost in a land which suddenly transformed from a paradise of easy living to a nightmare.

We have a new villa here. It is near the old French military Headquarters and was itself the French Officers' Club. Many an officer who laughed and drank and made merry in these rooms died a lonely death in the jungles at the hands of Asiatic fanatics and only 8 years ago .... I can picture the old legionnaires sneaking their lovely black-haired girls over the walls at night while on leave from the front. And where are they now? And the girls? The personal tragedies which have torn this country apart during the past 25 years are beyond understanding. Over here it is common for someone my age to have no family—to have had all your brothers and sisters and parents and relatives killed, and to have to prostitute yourself. A person could investigate the individual tragedies over here and never stop crying.

My orders finally came through and Tony Brush drove me to Tan Son Nhut Airport to catch a flight to Da Nang with connections to the Philippines, Japan, San Francisco, and Boston. My parents met my plane. Saigon suddenly seemed remote and far away.

PART III

The War at Home

My army commitment ended in November 1964. After I returned from Vietnam, in April 1963, I spent a year and a half in the White Plains, New York, field office conducting routine background checks on army personnel needing security clearances. Instead of talking to French planters and evangelist missionaries in South Vietnam's highlands, I was ringing doorbells in Westchester County and asking housewives if they considered a neighbor to be trustworthy and loyal to America. On weekends, through the USO, an army buddy and I would score comp tickets to Broadway theater productions, go to the horse races at Aqueduct, and attend tea dances at Cardinal Spellman's Servicemen's Club on Park Avenue. It was a far cry from Pleiku.

Of course, major events were happening—President Kennedy was assassinated, and the Civil Rights Movement was gaining momentum. As to Vietnam, when Congress passed the Gulf of Tonkin Resolution in August 1964, the war entered a new phase.

It was strange to follow developments in Vietnam from afar. While over there, I'd begun to see the futility of what we were doing, but now, as an ex-participant, yet still a soldier, I found the war at the same time difficult to support and hard to oppose. As the fighting escalated and casualties increased and we began bombing North Vietnam, I could only passively read newspaper accounts and watch television footage. When my military contract neared expiration, the army wanted me to re-up, even offering a generous bonus if I did. But I was sure that, if I did, I would find myself back in Vietnam for a second tour. I declined. Three months after my discharge, the place where I had been stationed in Pleiku, now named Camp Holloway, was attacked by the Viet Cong. Nine American soldiers were killed and more than a hundred wounded. On November 2, 1964, I put on my uniform for the last time and was discharged.

The army is like a mother, a strict and demanding one, to be sure. It

tells you where to go and what to do and even—not always successfully—
how to think. You give yourself over to it and it becomes who you are.
It wasn't who I was. After my discharge, I sublet an apartment on Manhattan's Lower East Side and, taking advantage of some savings, began
to write—first short stories, then a novel about an American soldier stationed in Vietnam who gets leave to go home and decides to desert. But
how do you conclude a story about a war that has not ended? I was stuck.
So I put the novel aside and waited to see how the war would end. But
it didn't. As years more went by, the situation in Vietnam only escalated
and grew more hopeless. I had a job teaching French and took another
working for a weekly newspaper, *Manhattan East,* for which I wrote columns and covered anti-war events, protest marches, and demonstrations
in New York City and Washington, D.C. By this time, I had become a full
dissenter to the war and joined peace rallies and marches both as a participant and reporter. For my articles, I was paid between twenty and thirty
dollars, enough to pay my rent.

Excerpt from a letter to George H. Hobson in France, dated May 2,
1967:

> *... I feel as if you left a long time ago, which is to say, not a few things have been*
> *going on in my life. I would say, of first importance, I went through a "crise de*

An anti-war rally in New York City's financial district on October 16, 1969.

Vietnam War protesters in Manhattan's Central Park, 1967.

conscience" a couple of weeks ago as regards America and what we are doing in Viet-Nam. There has been a total revolution (literal sense) in my political view and in my attitude since April 1962 when I was obliged to look up the country on an Atlas to discover where I was bound. Such a change, involving as it does profound dissent, is both intellectual and emotional. For several days, I was almost inarticulate with emotion. It culminated with marching publicly on April 15th and having to associate myself at least visually with some of the more loathsome, left-wing, mindless and morally degenerate elements which have espoused dissent.... I have been working up to this for years—at least two—and finally, conclusively, took sides. In the end, regardless of fairness, one has to be for or against, in other words committed. Whereas for a long time I have disapproved, now I am committed against American policy over there. And I am outraged by being associated (in the public mentality) with degeneracy and unpatriotism. An awful thing is going on. The espousal of the anti-war movement by irresponsible elements, a phenomenon hungrily capitalized upon by the news media, has distorted the attitude of the masses of people in this country regarding the issues of Viet-Nam. Witness the word: Viet-Nik. I saw the CBS news coverage of the last demonstration and was stunned to witness the disparity between what happened and what they reported. It was a distortion which seemed designed to discredit the peace march by overemphasizing any negative and unattractive aspect of it. CBS described the gathering of some 100,000 people in Central Park as thousands of young people "trampling down underfoot the sprouting grass." That is pure and simple slanting the news, something which should be unthinkable to the likes of CBS.

... Well, I shan't carry on any further about Viet-Nam. There is a madness running around. Behind the war one can no longer find reasons. The widespread

175

A demonstration to end the Vietnam War in Central Park's Sheep Meadow, November 14, 1969.

frustration is causing extremism. Push-button soldiers are being called our heroes. Even at good old stodgy St. Bernard's [the school where I was teaching] *a pro/ con discussion started around the lunch table and within 5 minutes the air was charged and the art teacher was calling the carpentry teacher a communist and being called a fascist in return. Commies and fascists at St. Bernard's! The country is more deeply divided now than since the Civil War. Who is to say what it means? A European I met recently said, "At last America is coming of age."*

The War at Home

Excerpts from a letter written to my sister and brother-in-law, May 1967:

Since I saw you, I experienced something of a "crise de conscience." And having done so, I feel once again a part of the world, a part of the human world. The regaining of this feeling, which came suddenly, made me realize to what extent I had been alienated, that is, grown alienated, during the past three years. Enough riddles: it all concerns what America is doing in Viet-Nam.... What's going on is insane. Suddenly I see it as a course of action ... which is not the outcome of those human motivations which are founded upon logic and reason. Just as a bigot cannot be reasoned out of his feelings by a comparison of negro vs white blood cells, the people who are carrying on this thing in Asia cannot be talked out of it. They are caught. They are beyond changing the course of their actions. They are burning up whole jungles and the reasons why have been lost and abandoned. No more justifications are needed. Some of them still mutter that we are invited guests over there. When we burn up the "wrong" village or bomb a company of our allies, it is referred to as one of the unfortunate mistakes which are inevitable. Now, they have gone so far as to blame the war itself on the people who have been dissenting from it. They bring back the #1 general over there to address a joint session of Congress (the only precedent being Douglas McArthur) and he says the people who are to blame for the enormous cost of human life are not the killers but the people who want the killing to stop. The strong insinuation is being spread around that disagreement with foreign policy is a thing for traitors and degenerates, or, if the person is of draftable age, for cowards.

... Within this country, the image of war dissenters is being built up to depict them as youthful and irresponsible, as moral degenerates (beatniks and vietniks, used interchangeably now), as communists and left wingers and so on. The news media, especially TV, emphasize the eccentrics in peace demonstrations. They zero the cameras in on every bearded face they can find, every left-wing extremist, every scuffle with police. Why? Eccentrics are entertaining. Police scuffles are "news." Revolutionaries are exciting. CBS is competing with NBC and ABC to have millions of viewers watch their advertising. It has to be entertaining. But in the process the truth is distorted.... I went to the march here on the 15th. Then I watched the news of it and could hardly believe the distortion. 100,000 peace demonstrators gathering in Central Park were described by a reporter as masses of young people "trampling down the sprouting grass underfoot." ...I went out and marched and it made me feel better because it was a symbolic act of disassociation. It was like a Catholic going to confession—he gets absolved of his sinful past. My feelings about it are so strong that they get the better of me in arguments ... on occasion. Well, at least I have taken my stand. I have disagreed for a long time. But disagreeing is different from being on one side or the other.

On October 21, 1967, as participant and reporter, I joined a mass demonstration in Washington, D.C., known as The March on the Pentagon. Afterward, I wrote the following account, which is excerpted from "Upper East Side on the March," published in *Manhattan East* [Vol. 8, No. 5] on October 26, 1967.

Part III

... The Washington Police gave us and four other buses which arrived simultaneously a motorcycle escort to the Lincoln Memorial. We arrived at 1:30 well-jostled by the seven-hour ride. The sky was clear, the sun warm, and the foliage green with edges of red and yellow. We were invited to march with Group "O"—Community Groups, but after putting in a tour in Viet-Nam, myself, I shouldered my way through the masses toward "C"—Veterans for Peace. The blue-capped vets made a tightly knit delegation in which I recognized men whose ages dated them to Viet-Nam, Korea, and World War II. Even the Abraham Lincoln Brigade (see FBI subversive list) which fought against Franco in the Spanish Civil War had a small delegation with a large banner.

Finally we got underway. The veterans marched to the cadence of several seemingly seasoned drill sergeants. "Hut-two-three-four, Stop this lousy war," was how it went along with, "What d'we want? PEACE! When d'we want it? NOW!" and "NO more vets!" Spectators applauded along the route. The crowd at the Pentagon rally interrupted its speaker to give us a long-standing ovation. A small veteran contingent continued past the rally and tossed copies of Stars and Stripes for Peace into MP ranks. At the parking lot delegates dispersed. Inestimable numbers of individuals, bored by the speakers, milled around uncertain what to do. They gravitated in the direction of the Pentagon. For myself, I found a tree, sat down, and consumed a ham sandwich. I had another hour to kill before the scheduled departure by bus to New York.

But around 5:30 I caught sight of a flow of people clambering up an embankment toward the Pentagon. Nearby ranks of U.S. marshals and MPs were ignoring the movement. I joined in and soon found myself on a wide roadway. Thousands were ahead of me. Then someone pointed to another current of demonstrators moving up a higher embankment. Up I went. At the top I discovered another mob, drawn up another road, being held back by a sparse line of marshals. And there behind stood the Pentagon itself, its roof dotted with soldiers. The marshals said, "No further." They were polite. They even smiled. And the crowd was friendly, too, in a very eager way. More and more people arrived. Then a curious thing happened. One individual suddenly sauntered between the guards and began striding up the road toward the Pentagon. The guards ignored him, choosing to stay with the crowd. But an officer halted him before he had progressed more than ten yards. They engaged in conversation. Then the man continued on. The officer told him to go back. But with a fearful eye on the crowd, he made no physical attempt to stop him. A cheer rose up and hundreds surged forward. That is how the demonstrators first got to the Pentagon steps. Within minutes thousands were seated before the inner sanctum singing "America the Beautiful." When a company of close-order troops issued from its doors, the chant of "Join us! Join us!" filled the air. And so it continued while numbers swelled.

Around six o'clock I sensed increasing activity in the rear and went back to investigate. First, I saw a civilian being loaded in an ambulance. Then I saw more soldiers. They were holding back new crowds at the same spot where the first wave had broken through. Many demonstrators stood just behind these soldiers, urging the crowd to do what they had done already. Someone near me spoke of tear gas. The air smelled of violence. I came to a personal decision that the cause of peace would not be furthered by pitting myself against Army troops. I executed a tactical withdrawal, clambered down the embankment to the wide roadway and found myself face to face with reinforced ranks of masked, helmeted troops. With heads enclosed by olive-drab steel, black rubber and large oval eye-sockets, they presented a vision of outer-space monsters. Someone tossed an apple at them. They advanced. I retreated down the last bank to the parking lot.

By this time, it was after six and dusk was coming on. Masses of people began searching for their busses. But no busses were to be found. Darkness fell gradually. Confusion grew. Someone at a microphone called repeatedly for the crowd's attention, but he had nothing helpful to say. Then the busses came, all at once, hundreds of them down one entrance to the parking lot. An immense traffic jam ensued. Night fell. People could not read their bus numbers. The loudspeaker beseeched everyone to return to the Pentagon to assist their miserable buddies. But the march was over, the people tired, hungry, thirsty. They wanted only a ride home. For two and a half hours I was caught in the confusion. The Upper East Side Citizens for Peace bus never showed up. Finally, I convinced the driver of another New York bus to take me along. We departed, leaving behind a scene of complete disorder and discomfort—thousands of people milling about in the darkness calling out, "Which way is Washington?" and "Where's bus 388 to Rochester?" The loudspeaker begging for wet rags for tear gas victims. Once on the highway I fell asleep. Hours later I woke up at Union Square.

Letter to my brother-in-law, Peter Heller, dated March 6, 1968:

... I think you overestimate Lyndon Johnson's support.... People are like sheep. They follow the herd, follow the leader. But they also want to be with the winner. Already Nixon is promising to end the war, though we all know how he will go about it. Also, people I meet have sympathy and admiration for the enemy. Even returning veterans; they call him "Charlie." Most of our field troops are on marijuana. I believe there is a fast snowballing opposition to the Administration. There ends my optimism for there is no alternative in sight. Also, I think probably the country is sliding into revolution. What will several million defeated troops do? Go to the polls? They'll go to the polls just like the blacks are. It will develop into a bad thing at every level. The writing is on the wall. LBJ is training the National Guard in riot-control; the black extremists are growing more revolutionary; the white conservatives are arming themselves. No one at any level has much faith left in the government. The Congress is made up of representatives, not leaders. The democratic process of social evolution is slower than the revolution of rising expectations. And more important than all, the madness of the war has caused disintegration of human spiritual and moral values. Again, I say it will all take a very bad turn.

I believe in what you say about taking up the pen. But only in principle. Personally, I can think of little to write that has not been written a thousand times already, written and read with indifference and inactivity. There are a few people who can do something by writing, but they are the most prominent and powerful. I confess I don't even read them anymore myself. What to do?—I don't know. But I have an idea what will be done. I got a sense of that when I joined the march on the Pentagon. What will be done about it is that the people will no longer put up with it all. They will go against Johnson and against the courts passively and actively. It has already started ... in fact I'd say it is well along and only has to be finished.... The leaders are in evidence, black and white, cast as "anarchists, communists, degenerates, revolutionaries" ... etc., by Johnson, Wallace and the others. So, as you see, Peter, I don't think we need to start anything. We have to make up our minds how to conduct ourselves in what is going on. This is a question of political morality. Do we revolt or counter revolt. Do we indulge in the historical inevitability of violence as a means for change or do we, with Yankee rectitude, cling onto our deeper belief in law and order, crime and punishment? I have not made up my mind. When I joined the great peace marches, I was filled with a feeling of pride in what was going on. It was the first stage of being swept up in a movement that will probably go astray. The damnable thing is that I am not an anarchist, nor a communist, but I believe in quick change. And I am getting quite intolerant of people who are on the other side. I suppose I believe in the greatest possible revolt short of the disintegration of law. I would hate to see the breakdown of law coinciding with the return of frustrated defeated soldiers and the resulting movement toward a military dictatorship. Such a thing is not by any means impossible.

From my journal, April 17, 1968:

I had a dream several nights ago. I was with my family at a skiing resort. But we were there in the summertime and were hiking through the woods. Toward the base of a hill workmen were dumping truckloads of fill. Already the shape of the hill had been changed by the great quantity of fresh dirt. I knew that the dirt came from the corpses of the dead in Viet-Nam—dust to dust, as it were. It had been shipped back in order to be put to an economic use, to improve skiing conditions for the leisure classes. I was choked with emotion and told Louisa [my sister] I would never ski in that place.

From my journal, October 24 and 25, 1968:

I heard Kennedy's "Berlin Speech" for the first time—it was on TV in connection with a Humphrey ad—and the effect of the speech and of the man, in contrast to the subsequent course of history in America, penetrated to my heart and brought me to tears. I was alone in my room and I wept like a child. It came upon me suddenly and convulsively and I curled over in my chair and let this grief and sorrow pour out.

And what is this sorrow? It is the sorrow which comes from losing hope. Kennedy personified the hope of my generation, the hope of youth. The energetic faith and vitality of my generation. When he was murdered an American history died and a new American history began to take shape.

We are living in a sorrowful day in this country. Presidential candidates draw up the dark fears and hatreds of a people. Olympic heroes raise their fists before the world in a symbol of racial hatred as savage and ruthless as Hitler's. With every gesture of hate the country continues to polarize.

When I saw John Kennedy speaking to the people of Berlin my heart broke open with grief. I felt the immensity of the loss that came upon the whole nation in November 1963. It has been five years and that sorrow lies stronger today than it did five years past. It is heightened by the true historical tragedy of that event....

How can I vote for Humphrey? How can I pull that lever registering a vote for this fussy little kewpie doll who has spent four years praising the Viet-Nam War?

On November 15, 1969, again as a participant-reporter, I joined a major anti-war demonstration in Washington, D.C., this one commonly known as the Moratorium. Estimates of demonstrator numbers ranged from 250,000 to half a million. During it, President Richard Nixon reportedly was watching a football game on television in the White House.

An article in *Manhattan East*, Vol. 7, No. 41, November 20, 1969:

THE NEW AMERICAN VOTE
David Noble

We left New York in the dark, Saturday morning, and rolled down the throughways and expressways to Washington. It was cold and blustery. The gray New Jersey farmland floated by under a sky of pale sun and dark clouds. I slept. When I woke it was snowing; the sun was still shining. Some girls behind the bus driver were giggling about the weather. The kid next to me said he had not seen snow in two years: he had just returned from a Far East tour of duty in the Navy. The next time I woke we were approaching a gas station in Maryland. There were a couple of "peace" school busses trying to turn off at the exit. A highway patrolman waved them on. We passed the gas station and restaurant. I made a quick count of over 50 busses. They were bumper to bumper the entire length of the exit and side by side at least two deep in both parking lots. When I saw the busses, something caught in my throat. I began to realize how many people were on their way to the Capital. It was like being caught in the current of a vast pilgrimage.

It was hardly warmer in Washington than in New York; Pennsylvania Avenue was several blocks from the bus station and I could see a segment of marchers going past the cross street. In the air I felt the bite of November and the electric thrill that surrounds parades: women calling together their families; kids jay-walking; girls running on the arms of their boyfriends. I reminded myself why I was there—to vote on the war; to have that helicopter with the camera record the top of my head. That is the new American vote. I used to watch army photo-analysts working in their labs. They would reach across their table-size enlargements with their measuring instruments and grid squares. They're skilled technicians. If they can count guerrillas moving under jungle cover, they can count my head under the Washington Monument.

I went down the street toward Pennsylvania Avenue and soon the chants and the songs reached my ears. They were marching on the far side of the avenue in the shade of federal buildings. In the white glare of sunlight, the banners were hard to read. Shading my eyes, I stepped around the corner of the avenue and the sight which met my eyes stopped me short. A strange emotion began to well up in my chest. To the left, a vast river of shuffling humanity stretched out of sight toward the distant Capitol dome. To the right, it moved out of view in the direction of the White House. My imagination had never conceived of such numbers.

181

Part III

I backed into a doorway next to a gentleman who looked like an Indian diplomat and from there I tried to grasp the significance of what I was seeing. It was like standing on the banks of the Mississippi. Where can so much water come from and how far does it have to go?

Fifteen minutes passed. A federal marshal along the route made the victory sign to some kids and shouted, "Three hours like this!" He was standing next to a city cop. The kids began to chant, "Police for peace! Police for peace!" The cop smiled, shrugged, walked down the line. Along the sidewalk, there flowed a steady stream of people who were going to the Capitol to join the march at its origin. For me, it was too far and too late. I decided to crash it. Doctors passed, radicals with NLF banners, a delegation from Kentucky, the United Nations, Canada. At last, I spied two smaller placards—IMPUDENT SNOBS FOR PEACE and EFFETE INTEL-LECTUALS FOR PEACE—and I made my move. At the first intersection, I looked to the left and saw a parallel march on Constitution Avenue. Somebody said the march had grown so big and had been forced to split. I was in only one half of it.

It's a long way to go to cast a vote—twelve hours and twenty dollars. My seat mate on the bus home, however, was putting in twenty-four hours and forty

Anti-war protesters at a huge peace rally in Washington, D.C., in 1969. Vice President Spiro Agnew referred to anti-war protesters by such terms as "impudent snobs" and "nattering nabobs of negativism."

182

dollars. She was from Boston where she had left her five children in the hands of her husband. He had wanted to come, too. She was sitting on busses for sixteen hours with layovers in New York to come down and walk the March of Death and go to the Washington Monument. There was rain and cold to contend with without sleep. And a forty-dollar tab. That's quite a lot to ask from an effete snob with five children. But another one I met had just come in from Texas. Leave it to a Texan to find such dimensions of impudence.

But that's why I went to Washington—to cast a vote on the war. Up there somewhere, perhaps in the Monument itself, a shutter clicked registering a minuscule measurement on celluloid which was my vote, anonymous, invisible to the naked eye, but for the first time since November of 1961, positive. The Moratorium was an affirmation of life.

People voted on many things on Saturday. There was a gentleman from the IRA. There were Buddhists in sneakers hawking pamphlets and dancing. There were less passive groups supporting somebody named Martin Sostre. But the big vote which turned out the masses was for more rapid withdrawal from Vietnam. That was the message that got through. For myself, I would have added something special about victory and defeat. I was not alone. One sensed clearly that a number of speakers viewed a new American triumph in the recognition and acceptance of defeat in Vietnam. For the United States had lost its first war. If you send half a million men into combat 13,000 miles away and you fight for six years and do not win, then you have lost—everyone has lost. We have failed to win on the battlefield; we have lost bitterly in the hearts and minds of people throughout the world; we have lost the esteem of our friends; even by the measurements of war, our soldiers are being perverted; our foremost national leaders are turned to extremism and put to ridicule; worst of all, perhaps, we are losing the precious soul of our nationhood and our youth.

To my mind, withdrawal is a term for defeat and I am ready for it. There is only shame in the continued pursuit of victory be it ideological or military. But there is a shred of honor left in defeat. Defeat opens the door to wisdom, maturity, and restraint. Only in losing can we begin to contain the arrogance which accompanies our power. Only in withdrawal can we put a stop to our slaughter of Asians. And after we live awhile with defeat, perhaps our souls will deepen and our spirits broaden. Then we can go about salvaging the shattered remnants of our national pride.

Last Saturday, we marched down Pennsylvania Avenue, turned a corner near the White House and came in sight of the Washington Monument. Once again, emotions welled up in my throat. For there on the sunlit hillside had gathered the masses which preceded me. It resembled what I imagine of the great holy pilgrimages of India. I climbed part way up the hill and sat on the grass. A voice came to us, it seemed, from nowhere. I asked someone where the speakers' platform was located. He pointed over the hill. I got up and walked in that direction. It was then that I saw the full extent of the crowd. An entire human landscape lay before me. The platform was a dark spot in the distance, the speakers themselves no more than ant-like specks. When Nobel laureate George Wald spoke about Lincoln and the meaning of freedom, his words were borne off by the wind. But when a young veteran stood up and said that if Nixon did not bring home the

183

troops, they would start coming home by themselves, the very earth shook as 250,000 people came to their feet. When Dick Gregory worried out loud about Spiro Agnew making a crank call on the hotline to Moscow, the landscape trembled with laughter. But when he paralleled the image of the vice president with the ghost of Senator Joseph McCarthy, a strange silence hung over those hills and fields of people. There is no shred of doubt in my mind that the New Nixon registered my vote last weekend. So did the Old Nixon. And even Nixon's Nixon.

It is a certainty that no president can take on the burden of defeat unless he is led to do so by his people. In the matter of withdrawal, the public is put into the ironic position of having to lead its elected officials. This began several years ago. It gained important depth with the "educational" public hearings of the Senate Foreign Relations Committee. It activated itself with the mass marches and demonstrations of 1967. Now it is spreading from the vocal minority to the silent majority.

The last time I went to Washington to vote on the war, the banners read, NEGOTIATE NOW; STOP THE BOMBING; BRING HOME THE TROOPS; GIRLS SAY "YES" TO BOYS WHO SAY "NO"; HEY, HEY, LBJ, HOW MANY KIDS DID YOU KILL TODAY. That was two years ago. In the interim we have seen negotiations, a partial bombing halt, a token troop withdrawal, soaring army desertions, imprisonments and draft refusers, and the forced retirement of a president. As one speaker declared, "If anyone here has any doubts about the effectiveness of the Moratorium, there's somebody down in Texas he can write to for information." Demonstration placards seem to be prophetic. But today, the placards all read IMMEDIATE WITHDRAWAL for there is nothing left to demand. American forces are clearly out of place on the Asian mainland.

To see so many people moving together is an awesome spiritual experience. One can, nevertheless, make reasoned comparisons with the past. Last week-end's crowd, besides being the largest demonstration in Washington's history, conveyed a different mood from two years ago. It had gained both self-assurance and humor. There was less noise, less frustration, and less romanticism. The violence which did occur later on at the Justice Department surrounded a radical splinter group which was protesting an issue other than withdrawal from Vietnam. Its exploitation of the peace march has been generally recognized. But beyond the destructive incidents, one sensed that the peace movement had matured since its march on the Pentagon. Mr. Agnew was the focus of humor more than anger and that in itself is an indication of maturity and confidence. When Mayor Washington assured the president that his police forces could handle the demonstrations, he was more in touch with the temper of protest than the experts above. The Moratorium, indeed the police, were good humored, affirmative, and well controlled. The subsequent condemnations by the attorney general of the entire peace demonstration in Washington is unfounded and testifies to the generally distorted vision of the Administration on matters of peace and violence. "The greatest test of the Moratorium is whether we can stop violence in Vietnam," said one speaker, adding that the United States Government is the source of the greatest concentration of violence in the world.

As the speeches began to drag and the cold to bite, I returned to the bus station. I paid my ten dollars return fare and climbed aboard. We arrived back in

New York after dark. I walked down Eighth Avenue and waited for a cross-town bus. People were huddled in a bank doorway to get out of the wind. Someone asked me how to get to Union Square. I saw a girl soliciting across the intersection. It occurred to me that at that very moment a soldier was struggling to live and another to kill. One day both of them would be recalled and mustered out and told to forget about it and find a job. I rummaged in my pocket for a bus token and wondered what they would do then.

Letter to President Nixon, May 4, 1970:

Mr. President:

I understand from news reports that you have dishonestly rigged a false public opinion poll regarding your invasion of Cambodia. This is an intolerable deception.

You may be sure that you have my unqualified dissent to the invasion as well as to the resumption of bombing inside North Vietnam.

I consider you to be a national disgrace. You are bringing dishonor upon this country. You are bringing shame upon patriotic Americans. What is more, your administration is pushing this country into a state of revolution. Only today four American dissenters were shot to death by your troops.

As a final word, do not mistake me for what you ignorantly call a campus "bum." I am an ex-serviceman, a Vietnam vet with an honorable discharge. Perhaps I am your silent majority.

David Noble
New York, N.Y.

Epilogue

Many years had passed since the war ended and I was driving along the interstate on my way to Albuquerque and the University of New Mexico. The parched landscape rolled by, the afternoon sun glinting off the hoods of pickups and tractor trailers. The juniper and cholla-studded plains reaching west to the Rio Grande appeared washed out in the intense light and heat. Shortly, I would be on a veterans' panel addressing a lecture hall of students enrolled in a class on the history of the Vietnam War. As I drove my thoughts jumped back forty years. For some reason, the high-desert landscape with its wandering dust devils brought to mind Saigon's humidity and monsoon cloudbursts and the mud and dust of Pleiku.

So, what to share about Vietnam with a hall full of college students? Had they even been born when the war ended? For me, that distant time consisted of memories, but for them it was history, something recounted in books, to be studied, to be tested on. How would they feel about meeting actual veterans of the war? I would soon find out.

To the astonishment of the three professors who taught the course, it had set an attendance record such that the University had been hard pressed to find a venue large enough to accommodate them all. Most of the students, I'd been told, had some relationship to the Vietnam War—a father who had served, an uncle who hadn't come home, someone they knew who'd returned maimed. The huge turnout showed how curious they were about this war, up until then, the longest in American history, undeclared, seldom spoken of, nearly eclipsed from public consciousness. For them, it was a shadow, little understood. One of the teachers had been an anti-war activist and one politically neutral. The third was Bob Himmerich y Valencia, a retired Marine colonel who, after serving three tours, had earned his PhD in history. The students had been exposed to all their viewpoints and now it was time to hear from the vets.

Part III

When I reached the flatlands south of La Bajada, the temperature rose, and I rolled down the car windows wondering still how to present my own experience. Maybe the kids' interest lie in why it started, why it lasted so long, how we lost, and who was to blame. Well, I would leave all that to the professors. For this session, all that mattered was that I was over there, and they were not and all I knew was what I'd seen and done. So, a few minutes of testimonial and then I would sit down.

When we think of colleges and the Vietnam War, we think of what happened later, in 1968, for example, when campuses erupted, and students burned draft cards and heckled soldiers and went to Canada. By then, protesters were marching in New York and Washington and San Francisco. Everywhere. The Democratic convention brought turmoil to Chicago. On television Huntley & Brinkley and Walter Cronkite showed us footage of wounded American soldiers being airlifted out of combat zones and hamlets burning and peasants straggling along dirt roads. We also saw bearded protestors waving signs in Central Park, masses of people walking down Fifth Avenue, and troops protecting the Pentagon from marchers. Americans had been confused by the war and taken a side and clung to it, like religion. "My country, love it or leave it." "Hey, hey, how many kids did you kill today?" Dissent was conflated with lack of patriotism.

I had become confused and angry—angry at the media for demonizing "peaceniks," at McNamara, and draft dodgers and students getting deferments. Even mad at my father for sending me hawkish newspaper editorials. At a family gathering, I walked away from a conservative cousin and World War II veteran who praised me as a patriot. When some young French people I met criticized me and America for being in Vietnam, I got so angry I walked out of the room. The French bashing Americans about Vietnam? *I* could do that, not *them*.

At the University of New Mexico, I found Professor Himmerich y Valencia's office, where the other panelists had already gathered. They were discussing weapons. I introduced myself and listened in. Their voices projected a mix of bitterness and nostalgia. Someone turned and asked what outfit I'd been in. For a moment, my mind actually went blank, then I remembered: Central Registry. There was no response—of course, it was our cover name. I corrected myself, the 704th Intelligence Corps Detachment. Blank looks again and the talk returned to tanks and malfunctioning M-16 rifles.

Since Bob was on the phone, I introduced myself to an older man in the room and he told me he had flown supply missions to the French trapped at Dien Bien Phu. That was in 1953, another war—no, to the Vietnamese it was the same one. In just my short lifetime, they had fought the Japanese, French, and Americans. And each other. And before that, the Chinese. War had become a way of life for the Vietnamese. No wonder their literature was filled with sad poems.

Bob got off the phone, glanced at his watch, and told us it was time for class to start. He said the students had been studying the Vietnam War in books and they were now full of anticipation to hear from us who had been there. We were meeting in the largest lecture hall on campus and he expected a full house. We were to go on stage and have a seat. Dien Bien Phu would start, then me, then the others in chronological order.

When we began to speak, you could hear a pin drop in the auditorium. I told some anecdotes and offered some personal comments on the state of military Intelligence in the early years. Then came the real vets. They gave vivid and painful accounts of their experiences in combat and then how they were treated when they came home. A long silence followed the last speaker, and I wondered what the kids were thinking. Then, like one, they rose to their feet and applauded us. It went on a long time. The vet on my left, who had survived the Tet Offensive, turned to me with tears on his face and said, "At last, I feel I've come home."

That comment seems like a good ending for this memoir. The trouble is, Vietnam did not end quite so cleanly. I had noticed a particular student—he was older than the others—who hadn't stood up and clapped. After class, he approached me and asked in a stone-cold voice to explain why he should consider me no less a war criminal than the Nazi murderers prosecuted at Nuremberg. For a few moments we looked at each other across a wide gulf. I was without words. He had listened to us but heard nothing.

We vets then went for coffee at the student union. As we walked along the path, one of them looked at me and asked what the matter was. When I told him, he stopped dead in his tracks and summoned the others and told them. They wanted me to point out the son of a bitch. I told them to forget about it, it's how it is. We walked on, and while we were having our coffee the student who'd made the remark came in and sat next to me. Now he kept quiet. Later, I asked Bob Himmerich y Valencia who he was. He told me he was the son of a career army soldier and he had torn up his draft card and gone to Canada.

He, too, had only recently come home.

Author's Service History

David Grant Noble enlisted in the United States Army in November 1961. He completed his basic infantry training at Fort Dix, New Jersey, and subsequently graduated from the army's Intelligence school at Fort Holabird, Maryland, as a special agent in the Counterintelligence Corps, or CIC. While at Holabird, he received orders to report to the 704th Intelligence Corps Detachment in Saigon (Ho Chi Minh City), South Vietnam.

Operating as a civilian, Noble initially worked out of the Saigon counterintelligence headquarters, located in a former private villa. In September 1962, with another agent, he opened a field office in the Central Highlands north of Saigon, in Pleiku Province. There and in surrounding regions, he collected intelligence until the end of his tour of duty in April 1963. His next assignment was to a CIC field office in White Plains, New York, where he conducted investigations of army personnel needing security clearances.

For his service in Vietnam, David Noble received the Expeditionary Medal and the Army Commendation Medal, with a citation relating to his intelligence-gathering efforts in the Central Highlands. He received an honorable discharge from the army in November 1964.

Since Noble always operated undercover as a civilian (GS 7), his actual army rank was classified. He was presumed to be an officer and always used officer facilities; he enlisted as a private and was a sergeant at the time of his discharge.

Index

Index

Index